*Therefore, since we are surrounded by such a
great cloud of witnesses,. . . let us run with
perseverance the race marked out for us.*

Hebrews 12:1

PROFILES IN FAITH

William D. Mounce

A Division of GL Publications
Ventura, California, U.S.A.

The foreign language publishing of all Regal books is under the direction of GLINT. GLINT provides technical help for the adaptation, translation, and publishing of books for millions of people worldwide. For information regarding translation contact: GLINT, P.O. Box 6688, Ventura, California 93006.

© Copyright 1984 by Regal Books
Published by Regal Books
A Division of GL Publications
Ventura, California 93006
Printed in U.S.A.

Library of Congress Cataloging in Publication Data.

Mounce, William D.
  Profiles in faith.

  (A Bible commentary for laymen)
  Bibliography: p.
  1. Bible. O.T.—Biography. I. Title. II. Series
BS571.M67   1984   221.9'22 [B]   84-9961
ISBN 0-8307-0984-3

Contents

A Teacher's Manual and Student Discovery Guide for Bible study groups using this book are available from your church supplier.

Preface

Oh, no! Another book about people in the Bible. What else is there to buy?

Yes, another book about our religious forefathers. But this one is different, and I hope you will enjoy learning from it as much as I have enjoyed writing it. It draws out truths in these people's lives and personalities which you may not have noticed.

To a large degree we learn by watching other people. This is why Paul tells his readers to follow his example (1 Cor. 4:16; 11:1; Phil. 3:17; 1 Thess. 1:6; 2 Thess. 3:7) as he himself is an imitator of God (Eph. 5:1) and of Christ (1 Cor. 11:1).

The ten men and two women we will discuss have a tremendous amount of advice and encouragement that will profit us all. Man or woman, saint or sinner, they all were raised up by God to perform a vital function in His redemptive plan. They will encourage you, frustrate you, teach you. They will show you what to do and what not to do.

I invite you to curl up in your favorite chair and enjoy their lives and personalities.

As is usually the case with authors, I want to take this opportunity to thank a few people publicly. My colleagues at Azusa Pacific University, Dr. Tom Schreiner for his interaction, and Mr. Bill Yarchin for his help with the Hebrew. My brother and his wife, Dave and Gini, for their gift to my ministry which helped make this book possible. And especially to Robin my wife, who provided illustration after illustration throughout the book; who typed each chapter as soon as it was finished so I could start rewriting it the next day; and who after three months of marriage willingly became a writing widow so I could meet the publication deadline.

Chapter 1

Abraham:
Strong and Weak in Faith

Scripture is the story of God's promises and His faithfulness to those promises. It is the story of how God made certain commitments to certain people, and then how He worked through people and nations so that His promises would be kept. Promise and fulfillment. The faithfulness of God. This is what Scripture is all about.

The story of Abraham is the account of God's promises to one individual. The promises are linked backward to the curse on the serpent, and forward to the death of Christ. Let's set the stage by looking back at the curse and then forward to how the promises were continued through Abraham's descendants. We need to know the playwright's prologue before we meet the players.

It all began in the garden: the Creation, the problem, the solution. The Creation: God created mankind with whom He could fellowship. The problem: We chose to sin, and therefore broke with His fellowship. The solution: God would destroy sin by crushing the serpent's head, and eventually receive the Creation back into divine fellowship (Gen. 3:15). The play could be titled "Return to Fellowship." Genesis 1–3 is the first act. Genesis 4 through Revelation 22 is the unfolding of creation's drama as God works to destroy evil and bring His promised salvation. Scripture is a record of how God was faithful to His promise in Genesis 3:15.

The structure of the early chapters in Genesis is a witness to how God worked. Genesis 1 begins with the broad picture of God's creation of the world and then centers in on one specific act of creation—Adam and Eve. The account of their sin ends the first act. The author then expands his scope to focus on the descendants of Adam and Eve. This account concludes with God's verdict that the individuals created in His image had allowed their hearts to become "evil all the time" (Gen. 6:5). Seemingly the only solution to this problem was to destroy the people and the evil they represented.

But what about His promise? God is faithful and therefore attention centers on one particular man and his redemption through the flood (Gen. 6–9). The author's focus then expands to all the nations descended from Noah (Gen. 10–11). Attention centers on the descendants of one of Noah's sons, then on the family of Terah, and finally on just one member of the family—Abraham. The stage is set, the players are introduced, and God's plan for salvation is partially revealed. When we look back from Abraham's viewpoint to the serpent we see that God chose to kill the serpent by making—and keeping—promises to Abraham.

When we look past Abraham we see that God was indeed faithful to those promises. He gave Abraham descendants even though his wife Sarah was barren. He preserved the people through the famine by sending Joseph to Egypt. He raised up Moses and Joshua to lead the people of Israel to the land promised to Abraham. In his sovereignty He brought Ruth and Boaz together and permitted them to become the ancestors of King David. God appointed Samuel and David to organize the nation. God raised up Elijah, Isaiah, and Jeremiah to guide Abraham's children. He empowered Esther to preserve the nation in a dangerous time so that it could eventually become a blessing to the world, just as God had promised Abraham so many centuries before. When God makes promises, He fulfills them. He promised to bless the nation through Abraham and He fulfilled that promise in Jesus, a descendant of Abraham. That is the story in capsule form. Now let us look more carefully at the man God used to establish the nation.

Genesis 11:26-29 introduces the players in God's redemptive drama. We are told that Terah had three sons—Haran, father of Lot; Nahor; and Abraham.

But the most important fact of the passage is in Genesis 11:30: "Now Sarai was barren; she had no children." The repetition emphasizes that God's promise to Abraham for descendants would not be fulfilled through human means. Sarah was barren. Rebekah was barren. Samson's mother was barren. Samuel's mother Hannah was barren.

John the Baptist's mother was barren. Mary was a virgin. Abraham's descendants are the result of God's special creation, for they were born from barren wombs. The nation did not evolve through natural means. Israel is therefore a witness to God's handiwork and His faithfulness to His promise to Abraham. The fact that Sarah was barren is no mere passing comment but the foundation of an extremely important theme that runs throughout Scripture—Israel is God's child; He is Israel's father.

In our age of numerous contraceptives and on-demand abortion, being barren may not seem that bad to some. But in times past it was horrible and even viewed by some as a curse from God. Children were a blessing and a security in old age. They were as arrows in a hopefully full quiver (Ps. 127:4,5). Provisions were even made so that if a man died without children, his brother had to lie with his wife, and the child born would be considered the child of the dead man (Deut. 25:5-10).

The story continues. Terah and his family left Ur but on the way to Canaan they stopped in Haran. They must have lived there for some time because they accumulated possessions and persons (Gen. 12:5). And there Terah died at 205 years of age. This was probably somewhere around 1900 B.C., give or take a century.

In Acts 7:2 we find that God called Abraham while he was still living in Ur. We are not told why they stopped in Haran. But we are given a hint. Genesis 11:31 says they planned on going to Canaan, "but" when they went as far as Haran they stopped. The Hebrew is ambiguous at this point and it is possible to translate "but" as "and."

The difference between the two translations is that "but" would emphasize that Terah changed his mind by stopping short of Canaan. We can only guess why he may have changed his mind. Terah was getting old and his age may have prohibited further travel. He also may have had insufficient faith in Abraham's call to continue. Abraham himself may have lost faith. It is a long way from Ur to Haran and there was plenty of time to think. And what we do know of Abraham shows that he vacillated in his faith. These types of things still prevent us from continuing in the Lord's will. We do not know why they stopped. But they did, and they lived in Haran a long time.

This became significant when God came to Abraham, in chapter 12, to renew His covenant. Abraham may have been living in disobedience to God's calling; he probably liked Haran. It was on an important trading route and later became one of the capital cities of the Assyrian empire. You could get rich there. Abraham was seventy-five years old and was settled in.

And then into this cozy picture came the unexpected—something that threw Abraham's plans and schedules askew. God sent Abraham a message that he was to move on to Canaan. God said that if Abraham would go to Canaan He would bless him. And in faith, Abraham changed his previous decision, picked up everything, and moved on.

Throughout Scripture Abraham is a model of faith because he left his home. But what is so special about moving? We do it all the time.

In our age of you-pack-it and you-haul-it, mobility is taken for granted. We want to visit

Grandma so we drive. We want to sit in Florida's sun over spring break so we hitchhike. If we want to talk to Mom we simply call her on the phone. If we want to travel to the other side of the world we can fly there within a day, or we merely turn on the TV and visit vicariously. Advanced forms of mobility and communication have made the world very small indeed. We can always go home again.

Not so with Abraham. Travel was very laborious; it was dangerous, it was time consuming, and it was uncertain, especially when you owned no land.

God not only called Abraham away from his land—away from his country—but also away from his family. Can you imagine how lonely and insecure Abraham must have felt? Here again, in our days of instant, worldwide communication, we forget that distance was once a great enemy.

God's call to Abraham was no trivial affair. He asked Abraham to trust Him to provide a new family and a new country, and for God to be his security. Abraham was to cut himself off from almost everything that meant anything to him and obey a God who in previous years he had not known or worshiped. What a request! What a step of faith! What an example to follow!

If Abraham left Haran, what would God do in return? He would bless Abraham. The word *bless* occurs five times in just two verses (Gen. 12:2,3), and the promise of blessing is repeated specifically to Isaac (26:4) and to Jacob (28:14). Abraham would be blessed with descendants and land. The promise of land is implicit in 12:1, explicit in 12:7, and repeated in 13:14-17; 15:18; and 17:8. The concept of a promised land underlies the whole of the first five books of the Bible. In fact, the other covenantal promises were dependent upon Abraham's descendants staying in Canaan. Jacob returned home from Haran, strongly resisted the move to Egypt, and insisted that his bones be returned to Canaan. Joseph's bones were also returned. But in order for the promise of a land to have any meaning, Abraham must have descendants. This is the second part of the blessing. And lying beside these two convenantal promises is the third promise of protection. Those who opposed Abraham would be cursed, and those who helped him would be blessed. These three promises run throughout the stories about Abraham and define the circumstances under which he lived.

But this is not all. Let's see this account in its larger context. Mankind was created, he sinned, and was nearly destroyed; but through Noah he was recreated. Just as the description of mankind right before the flood is a summary of that era of world history (Gen. 6:5), so the story of Babel summarizes the condition of recreated mankind. A group of people began building a city so that, through their own efforts, they would achieve fame and security. But they used only bricks and tar instead of stone and mortar—building materials which were totally inappropriate for a tower of such great size. So God scattered the people, thereby putting a stop to their desires which would inevitably have resulted in their further degeneration.

The people must have been wondering "What about your promise, God? Is this all there is? Have you scattered the nations to abandon them? What about your promise in the garden?"

It is within this context that we see the real significance of Abraham's call. No, God had not forgotten His promises. But God would keep His promises in a way we might never have suspected. As Von Rad points out, God chose one person, took him out of his country, away from relatives and family, and put him in a foreign land.[1] Through this one, solitary individual, God raised up an entire nation and would eventually heal the open wounds so visible in all the nations of the world. This is why God's promise to Abraham ends not on a note of personal blessing but rather on the universal note that, through Abraham, God would bless all the world (Gen. 12:3). This promised blessing is so significant that it is repeated in 17:8; 22:18; 26:4; and 28:14.

Abraham was one who by faith trusted God's promises and was obedient to His calling. Through him God would bring mankind back into divine fellowship. He gave up everything the men of Babel sought—fame and security. Abraham gave up his land, his country, even his family. He gave up his earthly security. And what did he receive in return? A promise. A promise that God Himself would make him great and that He would provide all the security Abraham would ever need.

God's promises deliver what the human soul so desperately needs. Abraham was clay upon the divine Potter's wheel, willing to be molded as the Potter desired, giving everything for a promise, trusting himself utterly to the skill of the Potter's hands. Abraham was one man, controlled by God, who shaped the face of the entire world. But the power is not in the clay; it is in the Potter.

So Abraham once again picked up and moved.

And what is one of the first things that happened?
A famine. There was no food in God's land of blessing. Talk about discouragement. He was promised
land, yet he was taken from his own. He was promised a nation even though he left his relatives. He
was promised descendants but Sarah could not
have children. And now he had moved his entire
household to a famine-ridden land. As we will see,
Abraham's life was filled with obstacles. But how
else can faith be measured?

Abraham continued to amass wealth and after
a while returned to the Jordan Valley just north of
the Dead Sea. Here he agreed to let his nephew Lot
take the lush valley for his herds while Abraham
lived in the mountains—definitely the less desir-
able of the two areas for the herds. But Abraham
was evidently a man of peace, taking the worse end
of the bargain so that quarreling would cease
(Gen. 13:8).

Consider the situation in more contemporary
terms. Imagine that you and your cousin are each
opening a gas station. Would you let cousin Bob
have the corner lot on a busy intersection while
you take the lot on a less-traveled section of road,
just to prevent quarreling? Remember that in
Abraham and Lot's situation Abraham was the
more powerful and did not have to make the con-
cession.

And what happened to Lot? He was taken as a
prisoner of war; eventually all of his possessions
were destroyed. What can we learn from this?
There is a hint in the text. The story of Lot taking
the good land concludes with the statement, "Now
the men of Sodom were wicked and were sinning
greatly against the Lord" (13:13). Lot wanted the

better land even though the people with whom he would be associating were very wicked. Lot's priorities seemed to be business first, personal relationships second. But when business takes priority over relationships, destruction is waiting to pounce. We are all affected by our surroundings. Although Lot was evidently not affected too much by the immorality of the people in the area—he resists their sexual advances toward the angels who came (19:6-8)—he paid the price of even being their neighbor. In most cases, however, the person himself will be affected by those around him—wife or husband, business partners, friends, or environment. All these take their toll on us, since we become like that with which we associate. If our business partners are immoral, we run the risk of becoming immoral. If we marry a non-Christian, our walk with the Lord can be severely damaged. If our friends are the "questionable" type, we too may become questionable.

And make no mistake. We are all susceptible to influence. No one is a rock—immovable, impregnable, unable to be influenced. We are social creatures, affected by our surroundings.

Of course, we should not stick our heads in the sand and ignore the world around us. Jesus did not pray that we would be taken out of the world but that we would be kept safe while in the world (John 17:15). Look at the choices made by Abraham and Lot. Abraham made the choice of keeping the peace. Lot chose the best location for business even though he would be living among evil people. As it turned out, Abraham was the successful businessman and Lot the destitute outcast.

Maybe we need to remember as we look at the choices these two men made that the Lord's prosperity is sometimes delivered in unusual shapes. Sometimes the relationships we establish are more important that the location of our business or the advice given by the business world. Abraham, the man of peace, chose what most consulting firms today would say was the worst possible choice but in God's providence it was the best choice. Abraham chose to strengthen his relationship with Lot. He had his priorities right and he was blessed.

How are your priorities? Is a godly peace more important than your promotion? Are you so sure that good business sense is always the right answer? Does God read the *Wall Street Journal*?

Abraham's rescue of Lot shows again the strength of his faith. Abraham accepted none of the spoil because it had to be clear that it was God who had blessed him (Gen. 14:22-24). Faith shows itself in actions and turning down cash in hand because of one's principles is faith indeed.

Most of the remaining account of Abraham's life concerns the fulfillment of God's promises for descendants. When the text introduces Sarah, the most salient fact is that she is barren, yet she is promised a child. Faith is the ability to say, "I believe" while staring into the face of impossibility. There has been no mention of the promise since chapter 12 and from a literary point of view, the tension is building. When will the promise be fulfilled? We feel ourselves sharing Abraham's excitement but yet frustration with the delay of the fulfillment.

Then in chapter 15 God repeats His promise

that Abraham will have a son. Abraham believed that what God said was true, and God "credited it to him as righteousness" (Gen. 15:6). This verse is the clearest description of Abraham's faith and is the climax of his life. The verse is so important that it is cited five times in the New Testament. What does it mean? *Credited* (also translated "reckoned") has its background in the Old Testament where the priest had to approve—to "credit"—an offering before it was given. He had to decide if it was a proper sacrifice. *Righteousness* is not primarily a description of an ethical state. It is "a term of relationship."[2] A husband is righteous in reference to his marriage if he treats his wife as a husband should. In reference to God, a person is righteous if he conducts himself properly within his relationship with God.

Abraham believed that what God said would in fact happen. This type of trust—in an unseen promise in the face of impossibility—is how we are to behave toward God. What type of man was Abraham? What can we learn from him? If we desire a personal relationship with God, the rules are simple. He says, "Trust me implicitly. Trust me totally. No matter what the problems are, no matter how things appear to you, trust me." God demands the same total, unreserved, unhesitating trust that a little child has for his or her parents. If you wish to be righteous—if you wish to behave properly toward God—this is what He demands. He requires nothing less. It is not who you are but how you trust. Trust like Abraham—total trust, despite the impossibility. Believe because it is impossible.

How will the serpent's head be crushed? How

will fellowship with God be restored? How will we
be righteous? Through Abraham we learn that the
path leading back to the fellowship of Eden is traveled by trusting the promises of God. And if we follow Abraham's example, we will be fellow travelers
with him on the road toward friendship with God.

There is much more we could learn about Abraham. Two final points stand out. Even after the
great pronouncement in Genesis 15:6, Abraham's
faith wavers under the weight of trials. He questions God's promise of land (15:8). He questions
God's promise of a son by having a son by Sarah's
maid (chap. 16). After another renewal of the covenant and a name change from Abram to Abraham
he still dared to laugh in the face of God's promise
for a child (chap. 17; see also Sarah's reaction in
18:12). And he questions God's providence by relying, as he did before, on human trickery in his
encounter with Abimelech (chap. 20).

The second point which stands out is Abraham's final test. All of God's promises are wrapped
up in Isaac. Yet Abraham is willing to kill Isaac
because he fully believes God will bring his son
back to life (Heb. 11:19). Sometimes it seems that
only parents can feel the full impact of this story.

The continuing idea throughout the story of
Abraham is that God is faithful to His promises.
God provided a ram when it was needed for the
sacrifice. Therefore, Genesis 22:14 concludes, "So
Abraham called that place 'The Lord will provide.'
And to this day it is said, 'On the mountain of the
Lord it will be provided.'" How true that proverb is.
How many emotional valleys have we gone
through? How many times have we needed help
when there was none to be found? And how many

times has the Lord provided when we needed it the most? If we stop to count, our lives become a record of the faithfulness of God.

Abraham was promised land, yet he had only one small field which he had bought. He was promised innumerable descendants, yet he had only one. And still he believed. He trusted God to be faithful to His promises. Is it any wonder he was God's friend (Isa. 41:8), and "the father of all who believe" (Rom. 4:11)?

Discussion Questions

1. Abraham is our model of "faith in the face of impossibility." He shows that if we want to have a personal relationship with God, then we must trust Him totally, implicitly. We must be willing to die, not seeing the fulfillment of God's promises, and still believe in those promises. Evaluate your own performance before God. What has happened in your life to show that you are in fact of Abraham and not of Babel?

2. Abraham is also our example of how strength and weakness in faith go hand in hand. What are some specific examples in your own life that show this same vacillation? Does God still work through you, even though at times you are unfaithful?

3. What are the obstacles in your life right now? Are they causing you to stumble or are they instruments of spiritual growth (see Jas. 1:2-4)?

4. What are some specific ways that you can help others to understand how much God was asking when He asked Abraham to leave home?

5. Have you been asked to make a big change lately—perhaps a transfer to a new location or a change of profession? Will you leave your Haran?

6. Is God making any promises that seem impossible? Is it as impossible as His promises to Abraham?

7. Do you sometimes feel that you are incapable of tackling a large problem? Are you denying the power of God to work through you? What are some practical measures to overcome this attitude?

8. Are you trusting yourself to be clay in the Potter's hands or are you trying to be the potter?

9. Are you a peacemaker, even when you are not forced to be and especially when it will cost you? What are some specific examples?

10. What are your priorities? What is more important: promotion or people? What has priority in the evenings: work or spouse?

11. God's blessings do not always come when we think they will or in the manner in which we think they will. Are you being patient? Are you being open to the type of answer to your prayers that God wants to send? Or are you insisting that He answer them when and how you want them to be answered?

12. What have been your mountaintops on which God has provided? How has He been faithful to you, especially when you needed Him the most?

Notes
1. Gerhard Von Rad, *Genesis* (Philadelphia: Westminster Press, 1973).
2. Ibid.

Chapter 2

Jacob:
Conflict, Deceit, and Faith

Even late in Abraham's life we can see that his faith was still strong. He commanded his steward that Isaac must not marry a Canaanite woman lest his faith be diluted or destroyed by the influence of his wife's religion. He also commanded that Isaac not leave the Promised Land—further evidence of his continuing faith in God's promise for land.

So the matchmaker went to Haran and the story that follows again confirms that God can work through an individual. God used one person—a steward—to continue His promises to Abraham, and one person to bring blessing to the entire world. Rebekah married Isaac. Sarah and Abraham died.

There are interesting similarities between Abraham and Isaac. Both passed their wives off as sisters. Both had run-ins with an Abimelech. But most importantly, God used each of their barren wives to show that His continued blessing of the world came not through human but through His divine means. Jesus came from a nation descended from barren wombs. Only through God's direct intervention would that nation and our Saviour have existed. But God is faithful and can give life to that which is barren. And so the story passes from Abraham to Isaac to Jacob.

Jacob is a man of contrasts. Once you think you understand his personality, he turns around and does something that seems totally contradictory. Part of the problem is that we only have snippets of his life and therefore it is necessary to read between the lines in order to draw some sort of consistent picture.

Nevertheless, there is much we can learn from Jacob, even in his birth. Jacob was a man of conflict. In contrast to the much calmer lives of his father and grandfather, Jacob seems always to have had someone mad at him. Even before he was born Scripture tells us that he was "fighting" his brother Esau (Gen. 25:22). After their birth they continued at odds. They were two totally different types of people with different personalities, different interests—they even sided with different parents. Jacob deceived Esau twice and had it not been for Esau's forgiveness—possibly achieved by God's sovereign protection of his elect—he would have paid the price. Jacob was always at odds with Laban. But who would not have difficulty with a father-in-law who lowered your wages ten times (31:7)? Evidently Jacob and his wife Rachel had problems (30:1-2), and we can only guess at the constant string of conflicts arising from marrying two sisters. Also, because of his sons, Jacob had troubles with his neighbors (chap. 34).

But not only did Jacob have conflicts with people, he even wrestled with God (chap. 28). Why all this conflict? We can only guess, but Jacob does illustrate how sometimes God's calling does not insure smooth sailing. As Brueggemann points out, God's election of Jacob over his older brother is the beginning of all the conflict.[1] In fact, God's election of the younger, in an age in which the firstborn was given priority, ensured a life of conflict. God's election of Jacob proved to be both a blessing and a burden.

Most of us are too much like Job's friends. "Success is from God," we might preach, "but conflict and troubles are the direct result of sin in your life and a failure to live a 'spirit-filled' life." Sound familiar? Problems equal sin. If you are being a "good" Christian, bad things do not happen to you.

Oh, whatever happened to the attitude of the early church which said "Amen" the loudest when it suffered? Whatever happened to our joy not only in suffering (Jas. 1:2), but joy because we are worthy to suffer for the Lord (Acts 5:41)? Why do we long not to suffer, when in fact if we do not share in the Lord's suffering we will not share in the Lord's glory (Rom. 8:17)? Jacob's conflict in the womb illustrates beautifully that God's will for some of our lives involves much conflict.

Jeremiah's life further illustrates this point. His preaching was hated by the nation and by himself; the prophet died a lonely, unhappy man. Maybe it is time for us to get off our success kick and to realize that God's will for our lives is not necessarily that we have a happy, conflict-free life. Maybe we have been selected to be vessels of conflict (see Rom. 9:22) to serve a purpose in God's overall plan, a plan which is much larger than ourselves. No, Christians do not always go around with a smile plastered on their faces. Life hurts, and even though we have the assurance of God's control and eventual victory, it still hurts.

Another lesson we can learn from the story of Jacob's birth concerns God's freedom. Can you almost hear Esau crying out to the Lord, "Why? Why my younger brother and not me? You chose us even before we were born. You didn't even give me a chance. That isn't fair!" But God can choose to break cultural tradition if in His sovereignty and omnipotence He so desires. God is free to do as He wills. Why was the younger Jacob chosen instead of his older brother, contrary to custom? Because God wanted it that way. Election is God's work, not ours. He can use Rahab, a prostitute, as a key figure in his plans (Josh. 2). If you were planning the strategy for the invasion of God's army, wouldn't you think it much more appropriate to have a godly woman hide the spies? Or, how about Cyrus? Isaiah calls him God's "shepherd," his "anointed," who will come and punish Israel for their sins (Isa. 44:28; 45:2). But why a foreigner? Isaiah's fellow countrymen could not believe that God would use a foreigner to punish His chosen people. But He did.

God is free to do what He wants to do. This message rings clearly throughout the pages of Job's life. Yes, God is consistent and true to Himself (Jas. 1:17), even when we do not understand what He is doing or why. He can choose to bless the world through one man. He can make vessels of wrath "prepared for destruction" if He so chooses (Rom. 9:22, *NASB*). He can even take a dead man, who was executed as a criminal in a matter cursed by the law, and through Him bring salvation to the entire world. God's action are not limited by our ignorance of His ways.

How many times have we cried out as Esau, "Life's not fair!" How many times have we complained when God hasn't behaved just as we thought He should? How many temper tantrums have we thrown when things were not exactly as we wanted them to be? Scripture gives two answers to this situation.

Habakkuk complained to God that the bad guys win and the good guys lose (Hab. 1:2-4,12-17). And God answered him, in effect, "Habakkuk, the bad guys will eventually lose and the good guys will eventually win. But I will punish them in my own time and in my own way" (see 1:5-11; 2:2-20). "Meanwhile, 'the righteous will live by his faith'" (2:4). "You must trust that I am just, and believe that I will eventually punish and reward properly." And how did Habakkuk respond? The prophet recounts the just and powerful actions of his God in the past and promises that no matter how bad things become, he will wait on God's timing and have faith in the justice of God (3:1-19).

The other possible answer to the question of God's justice comes in Romans 9. God chose Jacob over Esau even before they had a chance to do anything right or wrong (vv. 10-13). Is God unjust? No, because God is free to do what He wants to do, even if we do not understand. "Is that fair," someone might ask? At this point Paul puts his foot down and almost screams his answer: "But who are you, O man, to talk back to God?".

(Rom. 9:19). Paul can get hot. And when he is mad his writing swells up and bursts with scorn and indignation that a mere human would even dare to sass God. The passage is energized with a holy wrath against the assumption that anybody can talk back to God. Does anybody have the right to demand an explanation from God? Does anybody have the right to question—seriously, incessantly—the justice of God? Job did not have that right and he finally admitted it (Job 40:3-5; 42:1-6).

What is the difference between Habakkuk and Paul? When God behaves in a way we do not think is right, how should we respond? The whole key is in our attitude. If we, like Paul's audience, demand an answer, if we continually insist that God explain Himself, then we are in big trouble. God does not ask our permission or explain His reasons before He acts. On the other hand, Habakkuk's attitude is one of faith. He asked the Lord why and then obediently trusted in the answer which the Lord in His graciousness would supply.

Is life fair? Of course, it is, because God is a just God. In His way, in His time, the good guys will win and the bad guys will lose. But God's ways are not our ways (Isa. 55:8), and even His foolishness is above our wisdom (1 Cor. 1:27-29). We who would be righteous must trust, especially when we do not understand. Esau may have asked God why. When we do, what will our attitude be?

What are the Esaus in your life? Is God doing something now which you do not understand? The story of Jacob's birth helps us understand how we are to behave. We can ask why. No matter what happens in our lives we must trust that God is good and that He is in control. Even though we do not understand we must say, "I believe." And if we do not? The God of Job may come "out of the storm" and charge us with the words, "Who is this that darkens my counsel with words without knowledge?" (Job 38:1-2). Are you ready for that?

From Jacob's early life we can also learn that there are two sides to everything. And our point of view normally determines our opinion. Why was Jacob a man of conflict? It depends upon your point of view. On one hand it was God's choice that Jacob encounter some conflict. We have already talked about that. But on the other hand, from a human point of view, we see a different picture. Esau and Jacob were two totally different types of people. Esau was a hunter, a reckless and flippant man who, having sold his birthright, could merely shrug it off and treat it with contempt. Esau was also Daddy's favorite. But Jacob did not like the out-of-doors and was Mommy's favorite. The text says he was "quiet," but as Kidner points out, the Hebrew behind this translation suggests a "soundness" to his character. Jacob was "level-headed."[2] What a contrast to a man who sold his inheritance for something to eat.

There are two sides of the coin. Was the conflict between Jacob and Esau due to God's design or to different personalities? Both, probably. God often works in and through us, sometimes without our knowing it, bringing us to a predetermined goal. Yet, we ourselves are running toward that same goal unaware that God is in the running with us. Just as it takes both sides to make a coin, so we must see our lives both from our point of view and from God's point of view in order to get a complete

picture. You and I are not alone. God is walking
and working with us, whether we recognize it or
not. And when something happens to us maybe
the reason can only be seen from God's point of
view. When conflict comes into our lives it may be
our own doing or it may be sent by God to give us
an opportunity to work for His kingdom. Who is to
say?

Jacob was a man of deceit. This above almost
everything else stands out clearly in the stories.
Even his name has the figurative meaning of
"deceiver." And his theft of Esau's blessing is a
biblical hallmark of shrewdness and deception. He
listened to his mother, lied to and deceived his
father, and stole his brother's blessing. Isaac said,
"Your brother came deceitfully and took your
blessing." Esau replied, "Isn't he rightly named
Jacob? He has deceived me these two times: He
took my birthright, and now he's taken my blessing!" (Gen. 27:35-36).

But what happened to Jacob? He traveled to
Laban's household, fell in love with Rachel,
worked for seven years, and married her. Well, he
thought he did. But the deceiver was deceived.
Laban switched sisters on the honeymoon night,
and Jacob's only recourse was to cry out, "Why
have you deceived me?" (29:25). Laban's deception
enabled him to get both of his daughters married,
and also to obligate Jacob for another seven years.

But just when it looked like Laban had won the
upper hand, Jacob, the master of deceit, got the
last laugh. He deceived Laban by sneaking off with
his own flocks, herds and family (31:17-
18,21,26,31:26) without telling Laban he was
leaving. Rachel even got into the act by stealing

her father's gods and then tricked him into not searching her camel's saddle (31:35). The deceiver of the deceiver was deceived.

What a realistic picture. Deceit breeds deceit. Once the game is begun its flight is circular, bounding from one player to another player, back and forth, back and forth. It is a vicious circle with no easy escape. It is a game best never begun. Notice the irony of Laban's reason for switching sisters. "It is not our custom here to give the younger daughter in marriage before the older one" (29:26). Age has its privileges, especially then, and age should not be ignored. Yet, this is precisely what Jacob had ignored. He had ignored the primacy of Esau's age and had stolen what belonged to the older. And Jacob payed the price. Esau lost the privileges of age, Leah did not; and the deceiver suffered the same type of deception that he himself was guilty of.

Isn't God's handling of our sins often ironic? Doesn't He often turn our sins back on our own heads? Doesn't it burn us that much more when we are being done unto what we have done to others? Deceit seeks its own, and is usually successful in its search.

While speaking of deceit, we should mention Rebekah. The story of Rebekah pushing Jacob into stealing the blessing just begs for us to read between the lines. The sermons that could be preached on the dangers of parents choosing a favorite child are endless. Other sermons could be preached on the dangers of forcing timid children into doing things they do not want to do (see Gen. 27:11-12).

If it is indeed deceit on Rebekah's part, we can

see how that deceit turned back upon her head too. She urged Jacob to deceive his father. But it was only when he actually did, that she apparently realized that Esau would try to kill him and she would lose both sons, since Esau would then have to flee from the penalty of murder (27:45). And in sending Jacob to Laban, "for a while until your brother's fury subsides" (27:44), little did she realize that she would not see her son for another twenty years (31:38,41). Deceit breeds deceit, it turns back upon the deceitful.

But we should not forget that Rebekah was told by the Lord that Jacob would win out over Esau (25:23). It may be that Rebekah was fighting against a father's favoritism (25:28) and a son's timidity in an effort to secure the promises of the Lord. She may have viewed herself as working for the Lord.

But whether Rebekah was faithful or deceitful, God was still at work. Sometimes God works through people. Other times He works despite people. But whether our motives are pure or tainted, whether we are an instrument or a hindrance, God will be faithful. The question we must answer is, Will we work with the Lord, or will He accomplish His purpose in spite of us? Will we have the satisfaction of being the Lord's agent? Either way, God is at work. It is your decision.

Brueggemann points out that the Jacob stories in some places are almost offensive.[3] Jacob was a "rascal," and I am sure he was called much worse than that. But he still was an instrument of God, sometimes willingly, sometimes unwillingly. But God can use us, whether we fluctuate in faith (Abraham), or are downright deceitful. God's purposes "are tangled in a web of self-interest and self-seeking."

The question of whether Rebekah was acting deceitfully or faithfully reminds us again that there are two sides to every coin. And we have not seen the situation properly until we view it from God's side through the eyes of faith. Rebekah's motives may not have been pure, but they did fit into God's plans. Laban's motives may not have been justified, but it was Leah to whom was born Judah, from whom was born King David and eventually the Messiah. God's sovereignty over the world may be active in you even if you are presently fighting Him. But we must not take this for granted: "If we disown him, he will also disown us" (2 Tim. 2:12).

What else can we learn from Jacob? We see that there was one outstanding experience in Jacob's life that totally changed him. In his flight from Esau Jacob stopped for the night, and in a dream met God who renewed the Abrahamic covenant with him. The impact this event had upon his life was immeasurable. Following the experience, Jacob vowed that if God would keep him safe, he would worship Him and some day return to the Promised Land of his fathers.

From this point on we see a different Jacob. He vowed to tithe to God (Gen. 28:22), was very responsible and honest in his business dealings with Laban (30:33; 31:6,38-40), put up with abuse from his father-in-law (31:7,41), returned to the Promised Land when instructed to by God (31:3), gave God credit for his own survival and prosperity (31:7-9,42; 35:3; 48:11,15-16), and continued to rely on His protection (32:9-12;

43:14). He insisted on the religious purity of his family (35:2). And like his grandfather before him, even near death, his faith in God's promise was so strong that he made provisions for his body to be buried in Canaan (47:29,30; 49:29–50:14). This tremendous change in personality seemed to stem from his encounter with God in the wilderness at Bethel.

What have been your "Bethel experiences"? Have you encountered the living God? It is a changing experience. Two questions: To those who have met God—Are you a Jacob? Are you being true to your commitments? To those who have not met God—Would you like to travel to Bethel? Just as with Abraham and Jacob, so also your journey could change your entire life. It changed theirs. It has changed ours. It can change yours.

Discussion Questions

1. What are the conflicts in your life, both major and minor? What is your attitude? Are you glad you have been counted worthy to suffer for God? From what side of the coin are you looking at life?

2. What is your attitude when things don't go as you think they should? Do you give God hints at what He might do in this tricky situation? Or do you allow Him the freedom He demands?

3. When was the last time you asked God why something happened? Try to remember specifically what was your attitude. Were you demanding an answer? Or did you recognize that you do not

deserve an answer, and if one comes it is by the grace of God?

4. Specifically, when was the last time God worked with you in a situation? Specifically, when was the last time God worked in spite of you in a situation?

5. What steps have you taken to help ensure the purity of your children's faith, or even of your own? Again, be specific.

6. Have you noticed in the lives of any of your friends that their sins have come back to haunt them? How about yourself?

7. Are you siding with one of your children against another? Are you forcing them into something they do not want to do? Are you a Rebekah?

8. Have you been to Bethel? What specific changes in your personality have occurred since you met God at heaven's ladder?

9. Is your personal character such that your spouse can paint an honest picture of you and still have it evident that you are a man or woman of God? Are you as strong in character as Jacob?

Notes
1. Walter Brueggemann, *Genesis* (Atlanta: John Knox Press, 1982).
2. Derek Kidner, *Genesis* (Downers Grove, IL: Inter-Varsity Press, 1977).
3. Brueggemann, *Genesis*, p. 204.

Chapter 3

Joseph:
Innocence and Providence

Joseph is a joy to study. He never fluctuated in his faith. He was honest almost to a fault. He was almost too good to be true. But the beauty of the man is that he was for real. And the minor flaws that did exist in his character are almost impossible to see in comparison with his virtues.

The overriding theme throughout the story of Joseph's life is the providence of God. God made promises to Abraham and He was faithful to those promises even though it involved using the hatred of Joseph's brothers and the might of Egypt to accomplish His purposes. As far back as Genesis 15:13-16 we are told that Abraham's descendants would go to another land. The story of Joseph tells how those descendants went to that land and how God provided for them.

Joseph's story begins when he was seventeen years old and tending sheep for his family. He was Jacob's favorite son and he enjoyed and exploited this position. He wore (perhaps even flaunted) the special coat his father had given him. And he didn't hesitate to tell his family about the dreams that had indicated they would one day be subservient to him.

You would think that of all people Jacob would have learned not to openly prefer one child over another. But he blatantly shows his preference for Joseph. And the quarreling we see between Jacob and Esau continues into Jacob's own family. Many people just do not learn from past mistakes.

It is interesting to note that the sins of the fathers are often visited upon the children (Exod. 20:5; Num. 14:18; Deut. 5:9). Isaac favored one of his sons who in turn favored one of his sons. Jacob did not learn from his father's mistake and Joseph paid the price. For when parents sin, children suffer.

As strange as it may seem, we become like that which we detest. Any counselor can give you many examples—a father, beaten as a child, in turn beats his own children. You would think that he above all people would understand the horror of such treatment. A young woman marries an alcoholic even though her own father was an alcoholic and she hated life with him. Time and time again these types of things happen. We do not learn from previous mistakes; we become like that which we hate; and the children pay the price for our sin. That is part of the responsibility of parenthood.

Jacob's sons hated Joseph as Esau had hated him. And when given the opportunity, they sold Joseph into slavery. Joseph was sold to Potiphar who put him in charge of his estate. This is the first mention of a very obvious point about Joseph. He was an excellent businessman.

Potiphar, the jailer, and Pharaoh all recognized his ability and gave him tremendous responsibilities. Despite the Egyptian's disdain of nomadic shepherds (Gen. 46:33-34), Joseph gained their respect. Pharaoh even wanted one of Joseph's brothers put in charge of his herds (47:6) merely because he was Joseph's brother. Joseph must have been a tremendously respected businessman.

Notice that when Joseph first interpreted Pharaoh's dream he did more than merely interpret. He went on to suggest practical measures to overcome the famine (41:33-36). In a tight spot, with the pressure on, Joseph had enough presence of mind to suggest positive, practical steps. He did not remain theoretical but took the initiative toward application. Business needs people with vision and also people who can work with details. Usually a person is one type or the other. Joseph was both.

Joseph also worked for the good of his employer. No doubt he was rewarded handsomely, but his primary focus was on serving Pharaoh. Joseph succeeded not only in saving Egypt from famine but at the same time he enslaved the entire land and population to Pharaoh and insured him a perpetual tithe of 20 percent (47:13-26). Joseph was loyal to his employer.

Another point about Joseph the businessman stands out very clearly. Joseph credited God for his ability and success (39:3; 40:8; 41:16,39; 42:18; 45:5-10). There was no doubt in the minds of Joseph's associates that his success was due directly to the blessings of God. What an opportunity to give credit where credit is due. What an opportunity to say thank you to the Lord in a public way. People knew that Joseph's abilities came from the Lord.

Before leaving the subject of Joseph's competence as a businessman, there is one final point that needs to be covered: Joseph's age. He was a mere thirty-year-old when he ruled Egypt (Gen. 42:45).

Wisdom is no respecter of age; God spoke through young and old alike. Elihu's words to Job are tremendously significant and relevant. Job's three "friends" have said their piece. They have spoken from the "wisdom" of their years (Job 32:6), and their speech earns them God's disfavor (42:7-9). Then the youngster, Elihu, speaks: "I am young in years, and you are old; that is why I was fearful, not daring to tell you what I know. I thought, 'Age should speak; advanced years should teach wisdom.' But it is the spirit in a man, the breath of the Almighty, that gives him understanding. It is not only the old who are wise, nor only the aged who understand what is right" (32:6-9). Remember Paul's injunction to Timothy: "Don't let anyone look down on you because you are young" (1 Tim. 4:12).

There is a wisdom gained through the years. It is to be listened to and weighed carefully. But there is also a wisdom that comes from God which often is not a respecter of age. It is a wisdom that should not be ignored merely because God gives it to a younger person. Age has its message; younger people, listen to it. But the young can also have their wisdom and we dare not ignore it.

What else can we learn from Joseph? He was innocent. The story of his refusal to sleep with Potiphar's wife is the clearest illustration of Paul's admonition to Timothy: "Flee from youthful lusts" (2 Tim. 2:22; *NASB*). Joseph was a good-looking man, and it got him in trouble (Gen. 39:6). When Potiphar's wife propositioned him he responded with disgust and horror (39:8-9). "But how could I ever dream of sinning against my master and my God by doing this thing, for he trusts me with everything? I dare not betray that trust. I will not betray that trust" (paraphrased). Day after day she propositioned him and day after day he refused. But one day he made the mistake of being in the house alone with her; she propositioned him and what did he do? Did he stay and counsel her as we might expect him to do? Did he try to make her see the error of her way? Did they pray together? No! He ran like mad! Unfortunately, he lost his cloak, and with it she told a lie to Potiphar and Joseph landed in jail.

Flee youthful lusts. Joseph gives us an example which all teenagers and adults can follow. Run! Flee! Far away from sin. And don't look back! Running is not the sign of a weak person; not running is often the sign of an ignorant person. A man doesn't always stand up and fight. A lady isn't always polite. Sometimes the most manly or womanly thing to do, the most adult thing to do, the most Christian thing to do, is to run. Only a fool doesn't know when to run.

What else can we learn from this incident between Joseph and Potiphar's wife? For one, good looks are not always an asset. The world teaches us that appearance is everything; well, it is not. Joseph found that out. It is often a liability, and we need to be aware of that. Also, we can learn that one way to control temptation is to never let its foot get in the door. Joseph went into a woman's house alone, knowing the type of person she was.

Joseph also teaches us that the force of sin is directed primarily toward God, as he says, "How then could I do such a wicked thing and sin against God?" (Gen. 39:9). Christianity is a relationship. When you sin, you sin against God. You are not alone; He is with you. He has paid the price for your sin; it is the Lord to whom you are primarily responsible. Jesus tells us that when a sinner repents there is rejoicing in heaven (Luke 15:7). Certainly the reverse is true. Sin grieves our heavenly Father much more than it does anyone else. If you yield to temptation you are hurting Jesus, the very Jesus who hung on the cross to pay the penalty for that sin. We are not alone. Jesus hurts too.

Joseph spent time in prison for something he did not do. While there, two of Pharaoh's high officials were thrown into the same prison. They dreamt and Joseph interpreted their dreams. Was it luck that they were put into the same prison with Joseph? Of course not. The fingerprints of God's handiwork are all over the pages of this story. Joseph's interpretation of the cupbearer's dream was his ticket out of jail. It was God's control of events so that His promises to Abraham would be fulfilled. Joseph, the future protector of Abraham's descendants, was on his way to Pharaoh. From a human point of view, if Joseph had remained with Potiphar he might never have gained access to Pharaoh.

Two years later Pharaoh dreamt twice about the coming famine. The cupbearer remembered Joseph and brought him out of jail. Joseph interpreted the dream, was put in charge of the grain project, and was given one of Pharaoh's daughters for a wife.

Several points are worth mentioning here. Joseph named his two sons Manasseh and Ephraim. The meanings of both names show that Joseph still missed his home. Manasseh helped Joseph "forget" all his troubles, and Ephraim was living proof of the fact that God had made Joseph "fruitful" in "the land of my suffering" (Gen. 41:50-52). Every once in a while the author gives us a snippet of Joseph's heart. The man hurt. Despite all his prestige and power, he was still lonely.

Joseph was—and is—a model for those in power. He used his position for the good of the people and not for himself. Power is corrupting, no doubt about that. But there is nothing intrinsically evil about power. Power corrupts because people are corruptible. But we must recognize that those who have power can be agents of the Lord in accomplishing His purposes.

A final point here could be about the flip-flop nature of God's dealings. God does not always work things out as we might expect. Throughout the Old Testament we see God working through just one individual, unexpectedly. Who would think God would save Abraham's descendants by sending them into captivity? Who would think God would save them by raising up a foreign "gypsy." God is indeed a God of mystery. He will do what He wants, and will use solitary individuals if He so chooses.

The whole story of Joseph revolves around the concept of God's providence. Joseph's two statements about God's sovereignty show a heart of faith unequaled anywhere in Scripture. To his brothers he said, "But God sent me ahead of you to preserve for you a remnant on earth and to save your lives by a great deliverance. So then, it was not you who sent me here, but God" (Gen. 45:7-8). "You intended to harm me, but God intended it for good to accomplish what is now being done, the saving of many lives" (50:20).

The brothers sold Joseph because they hated him. But looking back on it, Joseph could see God working through their hatred. What better example is there of the principle declared seventeen centuries later, that "in all things God works for the good of those who love him" (Rom. 8:28)? God was faithful to His promises to Abraham. At times this involved the gift of progeny. At other times it was protection of that progeny.

Why did God choose to save Jacob and his family in this manner? Think of all the grief suffered by Jacob and Joseph. Surely there must have been a less painful way. We are not told why, nor are we expected to understand. We are expected to live in tension between what we see and the sovereignty of God. We live between our experience and our faith in the ways and wisdom of God. Our response is to believe and trust, enduring the tension—the freedom and mystery of God; the freedom to behave as He so chooses, the mystery of His ways. And we are to trust and obey.

The final point we should emphasize is that Joseph had no spite. Considering what he went through this fact is absolutely amazing. Can you imagine how terrified Potiphar's wife must have been when Joseph became the governor of all Egypt? She must have been shaking in her boots.

But as far as we know he took no revenge.

Even toward his brothers Joseph held no spite. At first glance his initial behavior toward them may seem to be vengeful and intimidating (Gen. 42:9,12,14). Many interpret him to be so. The problem is that three times he burst into tears (42:24; 43:30; 45:2). Spite does not cry. So what is going on?

Joseph gave the clue when he told his brothers that he would test them to see if they were spies (42:15-16). But in actuality he was testing to see if they had changed, if they were sorry that they had sold him into slavery. And there was also a strong element of discipline in this testing.

Had they changed? Most certainly, as is evidenced by two factors. About ten years earlier they listened impassionately as Joseph pleaded for his life from the pit (42:21). But later when faced with the safety of Joseph's brother, Benjamin, they showed a tremendous amount of concern. Reuben told Jacob that his own sons would die if Benjamin did not return (42:37). Judah personally promised his safety (43:8-10), and passionately pleaded with Joseph that he be enslaved and not Benjamin (44:18-34). Notice too that all the brothers tore their clothes when the cup was found in Benjamin's sack (44:13). Quite a change from the ten men who had cared so little for their brother and father that they dumpd Joseph into a pit and later sold him into slavery.

The other factor which shows that they changed is their guilt. Notice their reaction when Joseph first accuses them of spying. "Surely we are being punished because of our brother. We saw how distressed he was when he pleaded with

us for his life, but we would not listen; that's why
this distress has come upon us" (42:21). When the
brothers found the silver in their sacks they
responded, "What is this that God has done to us"
(42:28), evidently thinking this to be God's punishment for selling Joseph. When they returned to
Egypt after the cup was found, Judah confessed,
"God has uncovered your servants' guilt" (44:16),
referring primarily to their selling of Joseph, since
they knew themselves to be innocent with respect
to Joseph's cup. And even after Jacob's death,
they still feared Joseph's revenge (50:15-21). Can
you imagine what the past decade must have been
like for them, their guilty consciences gnawing
away at their souls? Can you imagine what a relief
it must have been for them to finally confess their
sin? The brothers certainly had changed.

Joseph was a man without spite. He recognized
God's handiwork even in his brothers' evil
designs. And he sought no revenge. How many of
us have been treated this unjustly? How many of
us have been in such a powerful position to get
revenge? And yet, how many of us have forgiven
like Joseph? How many of us live a life of no spite?

Discussion Questions

1. Can you think of any ways in which people
are too nice to you in ways that are not fair to others? What will you do about it?

2. Are you learning from past mistakes? Or are
you doing the same old things over and over
again? Have you acquired certain traits which you

have previously said you would never have? What are you going to do about it?

3. What type of worker are you? Are you as responsible as Joseph?

4. Can people see the Lord at work in you? Is His strength evident in your weakness? Or are you hiding the Source of your abilities?

5. What is your attitude toward youth? Do you automatically rule out people simply because they are young?

6. When was the last time you toyed with sin? Who won? When was the last time you ran full speed away from sin? How did you feel when it was over?

7. In what ways has beauty been a problem for you?

8. When you sin, to whom do you apologize first?

9. Politicians and people in power, are you working for the good of others or for yourselves? What are your priorities?

10. Do you have sufficient faith to look at a bad situation and still claim that God is at work in it? When was the last time it was evident God was working through bad situations? Is God being faithful to His promises to take care of you? Did you thank Him for his care?

11. Have people hurt you? Have they gone so far as to sell you into slavery? How do you relate to them now? Are you spiteful, vengeful? Are you going to get even now that you are in the position to do so?

Chapter 4

Moses:
Patience, and Hatred of Evil

The descendants of Abraham went to Egypt, and after four centuries they had multiplied into a nation (Exod. 1:6-7). The new Pharaoh did not know about Joseph and because of political fears he reduced them to servitude. Goshen, where the Hebrews were living, was a buffer area between Egypt and her enemies. If the Hebrews ever turned against Egypt they would make a lot of trouble. It would be like Mexico, a close neighbor with a large population, turning against the United States.

In a further attempt to control the Hebrews, Pharaoh ordered the murder of all their male babies. But the midwives refused because they "feared God" (1:17). There is much talk today about whether we should be obedient to the government if it is unjust. Here is an excellent illustration of the hierarchical ethic which says that the state is obeyed except when it contradicts God's law. Infanticide is definitely against God's law.

The real problem is not the theory but the practical application of the theory. When does a state law actually contradict God's law? What about killing Jews during the war? What about political or military intervention in other countries? What about imprisoning political dissenters? What about abortion? The principle is rather simple; application can be terribly difficult.

Throughout our discussion of Old Testament personalities we have been tracing the basic theme of God's faithfulness. Moses' life is a superb picture of that many-faceted faithfulness— faithfulness on both the individual and the corporate level.

God's faithfulness extended to individuals. The baby Moses was kept from being murdered or lost on the river. He was raised both by his mother and by Pharaoh's daughter. It is even possible that he was being raised as heir to Pharaoh's throne.[1] God's faithfulness also lead Moses to the desert where he learned how to live in that region as a preparation for the exodus. God's faithfulness brought Moses back to Egypt, empowered him to have the nation released, guided and gave him patience while in the desert.

God's faithfulness also extended corporately to the nation. Joseph's life showed God's faithfulness in preserving Jacob's family. On a much larger scale, the exodus shows God's faithfulness in preserving the entire nation. In fact, God's faithfulness is so evident in the exodus that throughout the centuries, it is this event to which the biblical writers refer when speaking of God's faithfulness.

So Moses was rescued from the river by Phar-

aoh's daughter, and through the quick thinking of
his sister, Moses' real mother raised him. When
older, Moses went to the palace and lived as Pharaoh's grandson. The story of Moses killing the
Egyptian gives us our first glimpse into his personality (Exod. 2:11-14). Despite his position in
Pharaoh's household, Moses still saw himself as a
Hebrew. Moses went out to seek his own people
(2:11) and he killed an Egyptian who was beating
a Hebrew, "one of his own people." Why did Moses
view himself as a Hebrew? (Incidentally, the name
Moses can be derived either from a Hebrew or an
Egyptian word. Whether this was intentional on
the part of Pharaoh's daughter or just ironic we do
not know.)

We are not told why he sided with his ancestry,
but the answer stands out clearly between the
lines. It is the result of his parents' instruction
during his young life. The story of Moses cries out
with one vital fact—the importance of parental
instruction during the early years of a child's life.

Young children are dry sponges, eagerly await-
ing the moisture of instruction, soaking up the
teachings of life. Remember how difficult it was to
learn Spanish or German in high school? Young
children automatically soak up languages with
apparent ease. Their eyes are floodgates, wide
open, taking in everything they experience. And
those experiences become the building blocks for
their personalities, values, interests, and goals.

What is more important? Our own interests or
the life of another human being? Whatever we
think about careers and such things, both for men
and for women, we dare not miss the central message: through God and our love we brought a life

into existence, and that involves great responsibility. Moses' parents accepted that responsibility, and the instruction of their babe lasted a lifetime.

When Pharaoh heard that Moses killed an Egyptian, he figured that his adopted son was siding with his ancestry and drove him out of Egypt. Is that what really happened? Of course not. God was faithful. We see His divine handiwork in the situation. He wanted Moses away from Egypt for a while to prepare him for the great tasks ahead. God works through good people, bad people, good situations, bad situations. God worked through the anger of Pharaoh to prepare Moses for the greatest event in the history of Judaism.

One final point deserves attention concerning Moses' flight from Egypt: he was faced with a decision. He could ignore the injustices of the time and live in rich and powerful splendor, or he could live a life of poverty and pain. In other words, he had to decide with which heritage he would place his loyalties. And what a choice he made. As the New Testament says, "By faith Moses, when he had grown up, refused to be known as the son of Pharaoh's daughter. He chose to be mistreated along with the people of God rather than to enjoy the pleasures of sin for a short time. He regarded disgrace for the sake of Christ of greater value than the treasures of Egypt, because he was looking ahead to his reward" (Heb. 11:24-26).

Not many of us are faced with a choice of this magnitude. But the choice of heritage is a choice that is made by all. Abraham chose the Lord "and he was called God's friend" (Jas. 2:23). Moses chose the humbled Hebrews over the exalted Egyptians.

Moses fled to Midian, married Zipporah, and lived forty years. (This happened somewhere around 1400 B.C. or perhaps a little later.) When Moses was eighty (Acts 7:23,30), God, in the burning bush, called him to return to Egypt and to lead the people out. There is much we can learn from how Moses responded to this call.

We saw earlier how Jacob had his "Bethel experience" after which he was a changed man. Unfortunately, we do not know much about Moses before his "burning bush experience," so we cannot tell how much the incident may have changed him. But the Moses we get to know was a strong, uncompromising, patient man. And his first meeting with God must have had considerable impact.

The most noticeable characteristic of Moses' talk with God is his continual whining (Exod. 3:7–4:17).

"Go to Egypt, Moses."

"But I'm a nobody, and Pharaoh won't release the people."

"I am with you; now, go to Egypt, Moses."

"But what is your name?"

"I am Jehovah, but never you mind; deliver my people."

"But what if they won't listen to me?"

"Here are three miraculous signs; now go to Egypt, Moses."

"But I don't talk so good."

"I will help you; be on your way."

"Oh, please, I don't want to go."

"I've had it with you Moses. I've told you to go. I've told you I will be with you. I'll even send Aaron with you. Now get going."

When we read the account, Moses' whining

sounds almost silly. But we should not forget what God was asking him to do. God wanted Moses to go back home where his adopted grandfather had tried to kill him. Several years ago it would have been like sending a Christian international student from Uganda back to Idi Amin.

Do we whine when God tells us to do something? Of course we do.

God says, "Have regular, daily devotions."

"But I have to be at work by 8:00 and I'm too tired when I get home."

"Pray to me regularly."

"I forget to."

"Witness to that woman."

"But she'll think I'm weird."

"Spend time with your son on Saturdays."

"But that's my only day out with the boys."

"Don't regularly do your normal work on Sunday."

"But I'm playing golf all day Saturday, and I still have things to do before Monday."

"Don't see dirty movies."

"But all my friends are going."

"Teach the Sunday School class."

"But I don't talk no good."

Of course we whine. When Moses whined, "the Lord's anger burned against" him (Exod. 4:14). Are you a whiner? Are you ready for the Lord's anger to burn against you? Will you test the Lord's patience? Or will you cheerfully obey Him the first time He asks?

As Moses stood before one of the most powerful rulers in all the world we can really see again how God often works through one individual, and how through that one person God's power shines forth.

God chose one individual, a slave, the son of a slave, saved him from Pharaoh's death, and placed him eighty years later in front of another Pharaoh, demanding the release of a nation of slaves. One person, empowered by God, can change the world. If only we could understand that, draw our strength from it, and do battle with the world. The victory is ours for the asking. God will use you to change your part of the world—maybe the whole world—if only you will travel to your Egypt. Moses believed and went. He knew that the power is not in the clay; it is in the Potter. Will you?

Moses went to Egypt and the first thing he accomplished was to get the Hebrews working harder. Pharaoh made them gather their own straw for the adobe bricks. Not very successful at first, was he? But God never promised us a rose garden. He never promised that the path He wants us to follow would be strewn with lilies. Rather, the path is cluttered with the rocks of disappointment, the stones of depression, and the boulders of failure. Moses went to help and he hurt the situation. And to make it worse, he had to watch others suffer for his own actions. That is much more painful than suffering yourself if you really care about the people. Moses hurt. He complained to God. He was rejected by the people. Not a great first day on the job.

And so the plagues began. Blood. Frogs. Gnats. Flies. Death of Egyptian livestock. Boils. Hail. Locusts. Darkness. The firstborn son. Things went from bad to worse to impossible. And throughout the whole story Pharaoh refused to let the Hebrews go. The author fluctuates between saying that Pharaoh hardened his own heart

(Exod. 7:13,22; 8:15,19,32; 9:7,17) and that God hardened Pharaoh's heart (7:3; 9:12; 10:20,27). Notice how in 9:34 and 10:1 these two thoughts are put side by side. Both are needed to paint the whole picture.

But note the reason why Pharaoh's heart became hard. Notice why Egypt had become great. It was not because they were naturally strong. It was because God wanted to make it evident that He is great and powerful. God is free to raise up an entire nation purely to show His greatness (Exod. 9:16; see also Rom. 9:19; Exod 6:7; 7:5; 8:10,22; 9:14,16,29; 10:1). He is free to do as He wishes. He is even free to have a person born blind for the singular purpose of showing His great power (John 9:3).

Pharaoh finally released the Hebrews after his eldest son was slain. Unfortunately for him, he changed his mind and his army was eventually washed out to sea. (Incidentally, someone may tell you that God did not really separate the waters of the Red Sea. It was only a marsh land, and Moses and the people just waded through it. This would mean the Egyptian army drowned in four inches of water! That's an even greater miracle.)

The people continued toward the Promised Land, complaining as they went. If there ever was a patient man, it was Moses.

"We want water," they complained.

"Here, God has made the water sweet. Drink."

"We want food."

"Here is manna."

"We want meat."

"Here is quail."

"We want more water."

"Drink from the rock."

"We want a god we can see."

(Aaron took care of that one.)

"The Canaanites are too big; we'll never be able to beat them."

"All right! That's it!" cried Moses. "I've been listening to all this long enough. Complain. Complain. Complain. All you do is wish you were back in Egypt. As punishment, not one adult who is living now will ever see the land. You will die in the desert." (See Exod. 16.)

Moses was tremendously patient. Are you? Moses put up with an entire nation of whiners for forty years. Think of that the next time your child whines and you get impatient. Moses certainly is an inspiration for parental patience.

There is much more we can learn from Moses, but space does not permit: he was a leader; he was an example of what Christ would be like; he was a workaholic who learned how to delegate responsibility (Exod. 18:13-24). But we should examine in detail two final points.

When we see evil, whether it be on TV, in the movies, in a book, in our friends' dirty jokes, or even in our own language and lives, how do we respond? Do we turn away and ignore it? Do we compromise and learn to live with it? Or, when we hear someone use our Lord's name irreverently, does our gut tighten up? When we see a dirty scene on TV does it make us feel dirty inside? How do we respond to evil?

When Moses came down from Mount Sinai and saw the people sinning, how did he respond? His "anger burned" and he smashed the tablets (Exod. 32:19). It revolted him.

When Moses saw the people's sin he actively opposed it. When Jesus saw the Jewish merchants making it impossible for the Gentiles to worship in the only place where they were allowed to worship, He actively fought against the sin (Matt. 21:12-17). Every time we are confronted with sin we must hate it, fight it, resist it, but never compromise with it.

The church today is in real danger of losing its hatred of sin. We dare not—cannot—allow this to happen. Sin must never become customary, natural, matter-of-fact. Our love for God and His holiness must remain razor sharp. We should hurt like our heavenly Father hurts when we hear His name used disgracefully. We too must throw down our tablets in the face of sin.

The final point we should look at has to do with Moses' face. Exodus tells us that when Moses came down from Sinai, his face was shining because he had been with God (Exod. 34:29-35). Paul picks up this theme in 2 Corinthians 3:7-18, and says that Moses veiled his face so that the people could not see that the glory was fading. And still in Paul's day the Jews' minds were veiled. But if they turned to Jesus the veil would be removed. "And we all, with unveiled face, beholding the glory of the Lord, are being changed into his likeness from one degree of glory to another" (3:18, *RSV*).

My father once preached a sermon on this passage, pointing out that it is possible to translate "beholding" as "by beholding" (i.e. as an instrumental participle). It was because Moses gazed upon the Lord that he was changed. Likewise, it is by gazing upon the Lord that we too will be changed into his likeness.

Nathaniel Hawthorne wrote a short story called "The Great Stone Face." It is the story of a young boy named Ernest. Across from his home stood a granite mountain which, when seen from a distance and from a certain angle, appeared to be a human face, full of wisdom, kindness, gentleness, and strength. There was a prophecy that "at some future day, a child would be born hereabouts who was destined to become the greatest and noblest personage of his time, and whose countenance in manhood should bear an exact resemblance to the Great Stone Face."

As Ernest grew older, he spent many hours contemplating the Face, and even though Ernest was an ordinary man, hardworking yet extraordinarily wise, people came from around the world to learn from his wisdom. It almost seemed that Ernest drew his wisdom from the wisdom of the Stone Face.

During his lifetime the townspeople three times proclaimed that the prophecy had been fulfilled in three different men. All three were born in the valley but lived their lives away from the Stone Face. Yet every time, Ernest saw that in fact they did not actually look like the Face. And each time Ernest was disappointed, because he longed so for the prophecy to be fulfilled.

Then one night while Ernest, now old, was speaking to the townspeople, a native-born poet who had achieved much fame and insight, seeing Ernest against the shape of the mountain, realized that Ernest himself was the fulfillment of the prophecy. Ernest was the Great Stone Face.[2]

Ernest had spent hours upon hours beholding the mountain whose human shape spoke of such wisdom and strength. He learned by looking, and his face mirrored that upon which he gazed. It is by keeping our eyes upon the Lord that we will be changed. Moses was changed. Ernest was changed. And it is by gazing upon Him, by keeping our attention fully on the Lord, that we will become like Him.

Abraham Lincoln said that after forty, every person is responsible for his own face. The point is that our face mirrors our soul. It is an outward reflection of what we are inwardly. Therefore, the object of our attention, that upon which we spend our time gazing, affects the nature of our soul and, eventually, our outward appearance.

When you look into the mirror, what do you see? Do you see someone who has been constantly gazing upon the Lord? Do you see someone whose countenance has been changing because he is seeing the Lord? Or do you see someone who does not spend time watching the divine Great Stone Face? Your eyes are the mirrors of your soul. What is the object of your attention? Are you changing into the likeness of God, or into the likeness of the world?

Discussion Questions

1. Can you think of five examples of state laws which, although repressive, are not necessarily against the laws of God? How about five examples of state laws which are obviously against God's laws? How about five on the borderline?

2. How has God's faithfulness protected you recently?

3. Husbands, are you accepting the responsibilities of a father and of training your children while they are still young? What are five areas of conflict between your private life and the needs of your children? What are two examples of how you have solved conflicts?

4. Wives, same question.

5. Are you a whiner? When was the last time you whined when God told you to do something? How do you feel about that now? When was the last time you gave "thanks in all circumstances" (1 Thess. 5:18) when you normally would have whined? How do you feel about that now?

6. Have you ever started a task for the Lord and been utterly discouraged after the first day? Were you surprised? Did it get better? Did you give it time to get better?

7. How do you respond to evil? Does it hurt or does it glance off you? What are some examples of when evil cannot overly affect you? What are some examples of when evil must sicken you?

8. What is the Great Stone Face in your life? Are you constantly gazing at the Lord? What are some practical steps you can take to fix your attention more steadily upon the Lord?

Notes

1. William Sanford La Sor, *Great Personalities of the Old Testament. Their Lives and Times* (Old Tappan, NJ: Fleming H. Revell Co., 1959), p. 55.
2. Nathaniel Hawthorne, "The Great Stone Face," *The Snow-Image and Other Twice-Told Tales* (Boston: Houghton Mifflin Co., 1883), p. 415.

Chapter 5

Joshua:
God's Leader

God is faithful. Through Jacob, God created a nation from Abraham's descendants. Through Moses, God brought that nation out of captivity. And through Joshua, He brought that nation into the Promised Land. God is faithful to the promises He made to Abraham.

But notice how long it took for God to keep those promises. Twenty-five years after God called Abraham, Isaac was born (Gen. 21:5). Jacob was born forty years later and lived more than 147 years (Gen. 25:20; 47:28). The captivity lasted 400 to 430 years (Gen. 15:13; Exod. 12:40; Gal. 3:17), and the Israelites were in the desert forty years. It was approximately six and a half centuries from the time God promised Abraham descendants and land until those promises were fulfilled. (In fact, scholars tell us that Scripture does not fully regard Canaan as an Israelite possession until the time of David, about 400 years later—see 2 Sam. 7.)

God certainly works on His own timetable. We may not understand why He takes so long to answer our prayers, but answer them He will. God's ways are mysterious. He is free from human designs. But He is always faithful. We must be patient and trust.

The most salient fact about Joshua's life and personality is that he was a leader. By studying him we can see how leaders are made and what qualities a leader should have.

How are leaders made? Someone once said that leaders are born, not made. Either you are or you are not a leader. To some degree this is correct. My sister's youngest boy, David, is only seven years old; but it is already evident that he is a natural leader. His friends want to know his opinions, and what he is going to do. But even David's natural leadership abilities had to be developed, strengthened, and refined. The same was true of Joshua. He must have been a natural leader but his leadership potential was developed by studying under Moses and by learning from experience.

Joshua studied under the master. He was Moses' second in command and his aide (Exod. 17:9; 24:13; 33:11; Deut. 1:38; Josh. 1:1). To prepare him for full command he was given some responsibility so as to learn to act responsibly, but yet not so much as to break him under the weight. Joshua was with Moses on Sinai (Exod. 32:17), underwent religious experiences with Moses in the tent (33:11), and was personally ordained by Moses (Num. 27:18-23; Deut. 31:14-23). He was fiercely loyal to Moses (Num. 11:28). In fact, he was so willing to serve under Moses that he allowed his name to be changed from Hoshea to Joshua (Num.

13:16). (Changing another's name is a claim to authority over the other; Joshua was content to learn within this type of relationship.) Joshua learned by watching Moses.

We all learn primarily by following examples; therefore, we become examples and teach those around us, whether it be our children, students, fellow workers, employees, or friends. We are all providing an example which someone else is watching and learning from. And we are, therefore, responsible for what we are teaching. Are we living up to our responsibilities? Are we teachers like Moses?

Notice too that Moses "encouraged" Joshua (Deut. 1:38). So many times our teaching involves either transfer of information or the negative aspect of discipline. "Learn this fact; don't do that." But Moses encouraged and strengthened Joshua (Deut. 3:28). In our own teaching it is absolutely essential to include encouragement and motivation. Jesus was not content to relate information. He motivated His disciples to do something with their new knowledge.

We have been looking at how Joshua learned by studying under Moses. Joshua also learned from experience. When he was leading the fight against the Amalekites (Exod. 17:8-16), Moses stood on a hill in plain view. As long as his hands were up, the Israelite army gained ground; but when they dropped, the army lost. The point was to make it clear to the Israelites that God was doing the fighting, and victory, therefore, belonged to Him alone. When the battle was won, the Lord said to Moses, "Write this on a scroll as something to be remembered and make sure that Joshua hears it"

(17:14). Joshua must learn from this experience that victory is the Lord's.

At another time Moses said to Joshua, "You have seen with your own eyes all that the Lord your God has done to these two kings. The Lord will do the same to all the kingdoms over there where you are going" (Deut. 3:21). Joshua's leadership potential was being molded by opening his eyes to what God was doing around him, and he was learning from those experiences.

This theme continues on the national level. The recurring phrase "to this day" shows that it was God's intention that the nation learn from their past experiences. It was also His intention that there be visual reminders of that past. Rahab still "lives among the Israelites to this day" (Josh. 6:25). This was a reminder of God's victory at Jericho.

God dried up the Jordan when the Israelites first crossed into Canaan (Josh. 3:14-17). As a "memorial" they took stones from the dry river bed and piled them on the bank (4:1-9). The purpose was so that in the future when their children would ask, "What do these stones mean?" they could tell them of God's mighty works. The purpose was also "so that all the peoples of the earth might know that the hand of the Lord is powerful and so that you might always fear the Lord your God" (4:21-24). "These stones are to be a memorial to the people of Israel forever . . . . And they are there to this day" (4:7,9).

They also piled stones over Achan's body as a reminder of his sin. It "remains to this day" (7:26). The tribes that settled east of the Jordan set up an altar of rocks as a continual witness to the future generations that they too were a part of the nation Israel, even though they were separated by the river (22:26-29). Ai was a "permanent heap of ruins, a desolate place to this day" (Josh. 8:28). The Gibeonites were still "woodcutters and water carriers . . . to this day" (9:27).

Why was there all this emphasis on piles of stones still present in Israel? Because people learn from past experiences; but where there is no reminder of the past, the past is forgotten. The stones were visual reminders of past events which were to be the teachers of future generations. Joshua and the nation learned from their past. Piles of stones reminded them of that past.

In Joshua's farewell speech, he recounted God's mighty deeds in the past and left them with this challenge: "Choose for yourselves this day whom you will serve" (Josh. 24:15). All around them were visual reminders of what God had done for them, keys that opened the history books, tutors for their children. And the reminders were visual, unforgettable. What are the "stones" in your house?

Joshua was a leader, trained by the master, taught by experience. He learned that success does not ultimately come from one's own efforts. Success comes from the Lord. It was through "the direct intervention of God himself."[1] that the Amalekites were destroyed (Exod. 17:14-16). It was only if "the Lord is pleased" with the Israelites that Canaan would be captured (Num. 14:8). It was through God's control of the Urim that Joshua was to make decisions (Num. 27:21). He was filled with the spirit of wisdom (Deut. 34:9; Num. 27:18) which came from the Lord. He enjoyed the presence of God (Josh. 1:5; 6:27). Success comes from God.

Take, for example, the battle of Jericho. Can you imagine how silly the Israelites must have looked to those within the mighty walls of Jericho? Reports had come about the fearsome Israelites, and here they were, marching around the city, blowing those silly trumpets. Yet Joshua was obedient to the will of God (see Num. 32:12). He knew that victory belonged to those who relied upon the strength of the Lord. And so he followed God's instructions exactly. It is easy to follow instructions that make sense; it takes total devotion to follow what seems like craziness. But that was precisely the point. The instructions were designed to be "crazy" so that everyone would know that the victory had come from the Lord. Joshua knew that.

As a spy Joshua relied on the Lord and claimed victory in His name (Num. 14:8). Even Joshua's own name shows that his help was from God because *Joshua* means "the Lord will save." He illustrated what the psalmist says, "Unless the Lord builds the house, its builders labor in vain. Unless the Lord watches over the city, the watchmen stand guard in vain" (Ps. 127:1). Strength is the Lord's. Victory is God's to disperse.

What an example to follow—not only for those who lead in a very public way but for each one of us as we lead our own specific group. Are we a leader of Joshua's caliber? Or does the size of our enemy take our eyes off the Lord in whom lies the victory?

The need for rulers to rely on the Lord has never been so great. Christians certainly do not automatically make better leaders. But if they are truly Christian, then they are open to divine guidance and instruction. This is especially true in the sphere of politics. Our political leaders must learn to rely on the Lord.

What about you? Are you relying on the Lord? "I'm not a politician," you might reply. "I'm not a leader." If this is your response, you have not been reading carefully. It does not matter who you are. Everyone is in some sort of responsible, leadership role. There is always someone following your lead, whether you are a politician, professor, homemaker, accountant, or blue collar worker. Someone is always watching and learning. We all lead our own little groups. The challenge is laid down at the feet of every Christian man and woman. How are you responding to the challenge? Do you rely on the Lord?

Christians therefore have a tremendous responsibility to pray for their elected leaders. Scripture does not say we should support only those we like (1 Pet. 2:13-17; see Titus 3:1; Rom. 13:1-7) it just says to support our political leaders; not necessarily agree with but definitely honor and support. (Remember that the government the New Testament says to support was evil, immoral, repressive, and definitely non-Christian.) Just as it is our leaders' responsibility to rely on the Lord's wisdom, so it is our responsibility to support our leaders by prayer.

Joshua the leader was tutored by Moses. He learned that experience is an able teacher. He learned to rely on the Lord. He knew how to follow instructions and to make important decisions (Exod. 17:9; Num. 34:17), and was not afraid to side with the minority opinion (Num.

13:30—14:9). He "wholeheartedly" (32:11-12) followed the Lord. Joshua began to accept the
responsibilities of leadership at a young age
(Exod. 33:11; Num. 11:28). As was the case with
Joseph, youthfulness, wisdom, and leadership
often go hand in hand. Joshua was also "strong
and courageous" throughout his entire life. He
was willing to confront and challenge his people
(Josh. 24:15), had a "spirit of wisdom" (Deut.
34:9; Num. 27:18), and was reverent before his
God (Josh. 5:14). Joshua also shows that leaders
are not always drawn from the social elite—he was
the son of a slave.

We have seen how Joshua was trained to be a
leader and what some of his specific qualities
were. The first time we actually meet him in the
text is at the battle with the Amalekites (Exod. 17).
The next time is his return from Canaan as a
faithful spy (Num. 13). The third time is at his
commissioning as Moses' successor (Num. 27:12-
23; Deut. 31:1-8,14; 32:44). In this ordination we
see yet another quality in Joshua's personality
which illustrates an important principle. Joshua
spent hours studying the Law. God says, "Be
strong and very courageous. Be careful to obey all
the law my servant Moses gave you; do not turn
from it to the right or to the left, that you may be
successful wherever you go. Do not let this Book of
the Law depart from your mouth; meditate on it
day and night, so that you may be careful to do
everything written in it. Then you will be prosperous and successful" (Josh. 1:7-8). You cannot feed
unless you are fed.

Notice the other principle at work in the passage: as goes the leader, so goes the nation. If

Joshua had not been obedient he would not have been successful and the nation would have subsequently suffered. When the leaders of Israel made a bad decision with the Gibeonites, the whole nation suffered (Josh. 9:16-18). Likewise, when one member of the nation sinned, the nation as a whole bore the penalty (7:4-12).

Not many of us lead nations and we tend to pass by these passages. But, as we have been saying, we are all leaders of some group or groups, and we can benefit from this passage. It tells us that all of us function in a social unit, and therefore our behavior will affect others in the group.

No one is an island unto himself; we are in the game of life together. We are responsible for the effects our lives have on others. Yes, in response to God's question, Cain was his brother's keeper. Personal responsibility has a much larger sphere of accountability than the secular world would lead us to believe. We are not isolated individuals, off by ourselves, with carte blanche to do whatever we feel like doing. We exist in society, and are responsible to some degree to the other members of that society. When we sin, it affects those around us, and we are responsible for those effects.

Joshua went from a slave in Egypt to a leader of his nation. Joshua is a good example of "pray and then go do your best." His military strategy was excellent. But yet, as his name indicates, his reliance was on God, and his victories were from God. Both prayer and work are necessary. We should not shift the balance. We can't just pray about something and not do the work, nor can we do the work ourselves and expect it to be enough.

Discussion Questions

1. When was the last time you appropriated one of God's promises and He answered your prayer immediately? When did He wait one month? When did He wait a year? Any longer periods of time?

2. When you were waiting for your prayers to be answered, what was your attitude? Does your attitude make any difference?

3. From whom are you learning to be a leader? How are they teaching you? Are you willing to learn from their example or are you fighting them?

4. Who are you teaching? Who is following your example? How are you teaching them? Are you willing to teach?

5. Are you encouraging or discouraging?

6. What has experience taught you about the Lord?

7. What are the stones in your house to remind you of the past? What is there that will make your children ask, and through which you can tell them about the Lord?

8. What has happened in your life recently that illustrates the principle that strength and victory lie with the Lord?

9. What groups do you lead? Are you relying on the Lord? Do you encourage your leaders to rely on the Lord? Do you pray for them?

10. How many of Joshua's characteristics apply to you? Can you side with the minority when you feel they are right? Do you pursue life "wholeheartedly"? Are you a loyal learner?

11. Are you accepting the responsibilities of a leader? Are you recognizing that your actions

affect those around you? What are some specific examples of how your actions affect others? Try to think of examples that secular society says are totally your own private concern.

Note
1. Brevard S. Childs, *The Book of Exodus* (Philadelphia: Westminster Press, 1974), p. 315.

Chapter 6

Ruth:
Gentle Strength

After Joshua's death the nation Israel went through a period of anarchy, and everyone did as he pleased (Judg. 17:6; 21:25; see Deut. 12:8). There was a recurring pattern. The Israelites would sin, God would deliver them over to an enemy, Israel would repent, and God would raise up an individual to defeat the enemy. A time of peace would follow, until once again the Israelites sinned and the cycle would repeat.

One of the more interesting of these individuals, or "judges," was a woman named Deborah. For whatever reasons, Barak would not fight Sisera without her help; so, together, Deborah and Barak defeated Sisera's army (Judg. 4:1-16). We also meet another woman in this section named Jael. She tricked Sisera into believing that she was a friend, and while he slept she hammered a tent stake through his head (Judg. 4:17-22).

Although there are not many women singled out in Scripture, those who are mentioned deserve special attention. We have already met Moses' mother and have seen the continuing influence she had on her son. We will meet Hannah who wept for a son; and Esther, whose daring saved the Jewish nation.

But during the period of the Judges we meet two special woman. The first is Naomi, who gives us a crystal clear example of how suffering can slowly grow into complete joy as God is faithful to His promises. In the first chapter of the book of Ruth, Naomi is convinced that God had turned against her (Ruth 1:13,21). But this depression turns into excitement when she learns of Boaz (2:20), to confidence that Ruth's situation will be happily resolved (3:18), and finally to joy when the child is born (4:14).[1]

The other woman is, of course, Ruth. Of all the characters in the Old Testament, few are admired as much as she is. Her personality, her commitment to Naomi, have long been respected by everyone who reads her story. She led no battles, conquered no foes. She did nothing that would stand out in the history books, except that King David was her great grandson. And yet, in a gentle way she was one of the strongest of people. The author of this book has painted a portrait of gentle strength, of a life that cries out to us: "Behold, the handmaiden of the Lord. Study my life. Follow my example. For behind every page of my story lies the hand of God controlling me, controlling circumstances, being faithful to His promises, providing for His people." It is a short story, teaching us of God's handiwork, of one woman's life from which we can all draw strength.

It was perhaps the worst of times. The nation

was in anarchy. There was oppression from without and famine from within. In this setting we meet a man and his family from Bethlehem, a little town five miles south of Jerusalem in the hill country. They left their home and crossed the Jordan to Moab in search of food, where they lived for more than ten years. Both sons married and eventually all three men died.

When Naomi decided to return home, her two daughters in-law wanted to return with her. Naomi's answer (Ruth 1:11) shows that she assumed they were thinking of a levirate marriage. This was a custom whereby if a man died without children his brother would marry the widow and the children born would be considered children of the dead man[2] (Deut. 25:5-10; see also Luke 20:27-33. The story of Tamar and Judah in Gen. 38 is also a story about a levirate marriage; see Ruth 4:12.) This was so that the name of the dead man would not be forgotten and so that his widow would be cared for. Orpah realized the impossibility of a levirate marriage and returned to her people. But not Ruth.

The text says that Ruth "clung" to Naomi and would not go (Ruth 1:14). The same word is used elsewhere to describe a man leaving his parents and clinging to his wife in marriage (Gen. 2:24). Ruth probably hugged her mother-in-law with such zeal that she could not be pried loose. And then Ruth said, "Where you go I will go, and where you stay I will stay. Your people will be my people and your God my God. Where you die I will die, and there I will be buried" (Ruth 1:16-17). The picture of love and commitment these few verses create is so pure, so powerful, that one almost fears to comment lest he dirty a portrait of tremendous beauty. And yet, to comment is our task.

Ruth was not afraid to touch. She did not stand there and plead with Naomi; she hugged her. Unfortunately, our culture today is mostly a no-touch culture. We must protect our own space. We dare not touch lest the true intention of our hearts be known. This is truly a sad state of affairs, for it is with a touch that a sister can most clearly tell her brother that he is forgiven. It is with a touch that a husband soothes his wife's troubled heart. It is with an arm around a shoulder that a friend encourages a friend. And it is with a hug when they part that a brother tells his brother that he loves him. These are situations when words fail miserably, for a touch is the linking of two souls. It bypasses the externals, forgets inadequate words, drops our self-defense mechanisms. It is a God-given means of expressing the true intent of our hearts when all other means fall short. The gift of touch can, of course, be misused, but even in misuse its power is obvious.

Ruth was not afraid to touch Naomi. This is not a call for public show of affection, it is a call to recognize the importance of touch, to understand the directness, intensity, and sincerity the language of touch can convey. When we were infants, the touch of our parents spoke to us of love, warmth, protection, security, and strength. It spoke much more plainly than an audible language ever could. Do you, like Ruth, speak this language? Or has it become like Greek to you? Do you need to relearn your mother tongue?

Ruth not only clung to Naomi, but fully committed herself to Naomi in words now famous.

"Where you go I will go, and where you stay I will stay" (Ruth 1:16). Much could be said about the need to verbalize our commitments. But perhaps one of the most important lessons we need to learn today is the value of actually making commitments.

Commitment has almost become a dirty word in today's society. "You are the center of your own world," society tells us. We have become anthropocentric. Yet, personal fulfillment lies not in an inward stare but in an outward vision. "For whoever wants to save his life will lose it, but whoever loses his life for me will save it" (Luke 9:24). Strength for salvation lies in a committed relationship with God. The same holds true on the level of personal relationships. The way to happiness and personal fulfillment is not the inward road of self-seeking and self-centeredness. The secret is in commitments made and commitments kept to others.

The church should lament bitterly the state of marriage today, especially within the church itself. What used to be almost foreign is now commonplace. Marriages are dissolving all around us. Why? Without being simplistic, the reason is best illustrated by a current wedding vow: "Until love doth depart." If only in the sphere of marriage we could grasp the truth given us by Ruth. Ruth's relationship to Naomi was based on a commitment of her will, and only death could sever that bond. That is why their relationship lasted.

Robin, my wife, and I have a saying. There are times when we do not like each other all that much. But no matter what happens, we will always love each other. Feelings come and go, but a firm, mature commitment will never die. I will love Robin forever, because our relationship is based on a commitment of our wills, and not on fluctuating feelings.

The book of Ruth divides into four tidy units. Chapter 1 introduces us to Naomi and Ruth and their plight. It concludes with their return to Bethlehem at the beginning of the harvest season. Chapter 2 introduces us to Boaz, and the plot thickens. Boaz was a rich relative. It just so happens that it was his field where Ruth went to harvest the barley. (Jewish law said that the harvesters should leave grain on the edges of the field so that the poor could gather some to eat; Lev. 19:9; 23:22.) They met, and Boaz showed himself to be an unusually gracious and caring man. He had heard of Ruth's good reputation and provided her lunch and promised her continued protection as she harvested. That evening, Ruth returned and told Naomi of her good fortune.

Chapter 3 is one of the more unusual stories in the Old Testament. It is based on the law of next-of-kin whereby the closest male relative was responsible for a young widow if there was no brother-in-law. In those days a woman could not just go out and get a job. Either her family would take care of her or she would be forced into a life of prostitution. (Incidentally, the same Hebrew word lies behind the English translations "redeem" and "kinsman." Boaz is the kinsman who is to redeem Ruth from her life of poverty and widowhood.)

Chapter 3 starts with Naomi playing the first woman matchmaker on record. Ruth needed to be provided for, and so Naomi told her to make herself pretty, go to where Boaz had been working, and after he had eaten and drunk his fill, lift his clothing off his feet and lie down.

It is very difficult to know precisely what happened here. We are dealing with ancient customs and with language capable of double meanings. But one thing is for sure: Ruth was not immoral. Throughout the book she is pictured as a completely virtuous woman. Naomi told her to do it, and Boaz's reply in verses 10 and 11 proves that she was not immoral. What Ruth did was to confront Boaz with his responsibility as next of kin, and may have gone so far as to ask him to marry her. (Campbell argues that her request to "spread the corner of your garment over me, since you are a kinsman-redeemer" (3:9) is a request for marriage. This argument is based on the similarity of imagery in Ezekiel 16:8, and on ancient and modern Arabic customs.)[3] Boaz may have been flattered that Ruth had not asked one of the younger men, and promised to follow upon her request in the morning. She left early the next morning, before anybody could recognize her, with a shawl full of grain so that if she were seen it would appear she had risen early to work. This was so that nobody would think she was being immoral.

Have you ever found yourself in a situation in which you are totally innocent but it looks as if you have done something wrong or immoral? Isn't it frustrating? How about the time you stayed up late talking to a member of the opposite sex, and when you walked home with that person you got those accusing stares? The best way, of course, not to have this problem is to be sensitive to how your actions appear and to stay out of those situations. But if you get trapped in a sticky situation,

Ruth teaches us to be sensitive to how it appears. Ruth and Boaz show a concern for appearances that we would do well to copy. As Paul says, reject "all that has a look of evil about it" (1 Thess. 5:22, *Knox*).

Chapter 3 is really the climax of the story. Boaz was a man of character, and once we read that he committed himself to Ruth we can sit back comfortably. Yet there is one little problem and the formalities are yet to come. Thus, chapter 4 delays the conclusion. Boaz was not the nearest of kin, and the nearest must be given a chance to "redeem" Ruth. They all met at the town gate where business was carried out in those days. And the business began.

Naomi, Boaz said, was selling her piece of property. Since in those days the land should remain "in the family," it was up to the nearest of kin to buy that property. Yet, with the property came Ruth, and that was the problem. The children that would then be born to Ruth would be viewed as the offspring of Kilion, Ruth's first husband, and not of the kinsman. They would inherit along with the other children of the kinsman and divide the property between the two families. This was too much of a financial strain and the man withdrew, leaving Boaz next in line to marry Ruth. This was, of course, what Boaz wanted all along.

Boaz and Ruth married and had a son named Obed. Obed's son was Jesse whose son was King David, the "father" of the Messiah.

We learned earlier that Ruth had a gentle strength. We need to read a little between the lines to see this, but it is there. She had a strength of character that drove her to make a commitment to

leave her home, her country, her people, and to go
to a strange land with an older woman who had no
means of support and would only be a financial
burden (see Ruth 2:11). And yet she went, never
wavering in her commitment to Naomi. She took
the initiative to collect food from the field (2:2).
She was polite; she did not demand her rights but
asked permission to harvest along the edges of the
field (2:7). She was an extremely diligent and
untiring worker (2:7). When Boaz showed her
favor she responded in true modesty and innocent
amazement (2:10). She conducted herself always
in such a proper and noble sense that her reputation was impeccable (2:11; 3:11; 4:15). She was
gracious in her speech (2:13), and was so thought-
ful that she even kept what was left over from
lunch and brought it to Naomi (2:18). When
Naomi told her to go to Boaz in a manner which
may be construed as compromising, not only did
she permit her mother-in-law to go husband hunting for her but she was fully obedient to the point
of challenging Boaz with his obligation (3:9). Ruth
must have been a woman of strong character.

And yet, throughout the entire story we get the
feeling that Ruth's strength of character showed
itself quietly. She put up no opposition. She never
complained or argued except when Naomi wanted
her to leave. She did not need to be told to gather
grain but just went and did it. Her innocence
when meeting Boaz speaks of a quiet spirit (2:10).
Her strength was quiet but unfaltering.

There are many other interesting characters in
the story. Naomi must have been quite a woman,
seeking the best for her daughter-in-law, encouraging her to remarry. Boaz too must have been a

very godly man. Scholars tell us that a purpose of the book is to give us paradigms of proper behavior such that in its characters we can see how God acts toward us, and how we are to act toward those in our community. Ruth and Boaz are certainly paradigms of godly behavior.

But the main character of the play never comes on stage. He is in the wings, directing the players, controlling the backdrop to the story. It is not "by luck" that Ruth found herself in Boaz's field (2:3); Boaz did not just "happen" to ask who Ruth was (2:5); the near kinsman did not "coincidentally" walk by the city gate (4:1); and when Naomi told Ruth to sit back, relax, and wait for Boaz to do his job (3:18), there is no question in our mind that the job would get done. Why? Because the main character of the play is in the wings, directing the circumstances, controlling the situations.

Who is the main actor? It is the same person who made sure there was a ram caught in the thicket for Abraham. It is the same person who made sure Esau was gone hunting long enough for Jacob to receive Isaac's blessing. He also is the one who had Joseph, the cupbearer, and the baker all put in the same jail. He also made sure Pharaoh's daughter found the baby Moses.

The main Actor in the book of Ruth is God. We rarely actually see Him, but He is there, always. His sovereign control of events, mundane as they may seem, are always His tools for shaping mankind and history. God dries up the Red Seas in our lives from time to time; He does do mighty deeds. But more often He is at work in the day-to-day affairs of our lives. Often we meet people, go to places, are late for appointments, miss cabs, because God is standing in the wings, controlling the events as our lives are acted out on life's stage. God is ever-present in the little things of life.

Discussion Questions

1. What do you think about this "touching" business? Does it hold true, to some extent, for everyone?

2. Give two instances in your experience where a touch from someone meant much more than words could ever have conveyed. Give an instance in which you wished the person had simply touched you instead of talked. Give an instance in which you now wished you had touched the other person.

3. What are three specific examples of commitments that you as a Christian should be willing to make but that the world says we should not.

4. In what specific ways have the commitments in your marriage or friendships carried you through troubled times? Would the relationship have made it if there had been no commitment?

5. What specific advice will you give your children or friends about commitments as they approach marriage?

6. What was an instance in your life in which you appeared to be doing something wrong when, in fact, you were not? How could you have avoided the situation? How did you handle it?

7. Which of Ruth's specific qualities stand out the most to you? Which ones would you like the most for yourself?

8. Are you as good a mother-in-law as Naomi?

Do you seek the best for your daughter-in-law? Or are you looking out for your little boy or yourself?

9. Are you as good a daughter-in-law as Ruth? Would you be willing to support your mother-in-law as Ruth supported Naomi if it were necessary?

10. Think of two mundane areas in your life where God's work through you has yielded important results.

Notes
1. See Edward F. Campbell, Jr., *Ruth* (New York: Doubleday & Co., Inc., 1975), for discussion on this subject.
2. See William S. LaSor, *Great Personalities of the Old Testament* (Old Tappan, NJ: Fleming H. Revell Co., 1959), for discussion on this subject.
3. Campbell, *Ruth*, p. 123.

Chapter 7

Samuel: God's Man in Difficult Times

It was sometime around 1000 B.C. and things were not getting any better. It was the period of the judges, a little later than Ruth and right before Saul became king. Eli was the ruling judge and things were still basically in chaos.

The book of 1 Samuel begins here. It shows that Samuel, the last of the judges, the next prophet after Moses, was chosen by God to be the pivotal character in this important time. It was a transitional time when Israel went from being a loose confederation of blood-related tribes to being an organized kingdom ruled by a king. (LaSor likens it to the thirteen colonies being organized into the United States.)[1] The transition was both difficult and essential. It was difficult because the tribes were descendants of slaves, not used to organizing themselves; and they had lived in relative anarchy for several hundred years. The transition was essential because in order for Abraham's descendants to be a blessing to the world, as God had promised, they had to be an organized nation.

Hannah, Samuel's mother, was very special. She was childless, yet wanted children so badly that she wept before the Lord. Her praying was so intense that Eli thought she was drunk. How many of us have prayed so intensely that our fervor could be mistaken for drunkenness or perhaps a mental or nervous disorder? Many of us are afraid to sweat, afraid to get in there and get our hands dirty. Instead of praying fervently, we would rather sit back and watch others play the game. But not Jesus. At Gethsemane He prayed so hard that He was sweating (Luke 22:44; see Luke 18:1-8). Are our prayers this intense?

Hannah's prayer was that if the Lord would give her a son, she would give him back to the Lord's service as a Nazirite (1 Sam. 1:11). This meant that Samuel never drank wine, cut his hair, nor ever went near a dead body (Num. 6:1-8). Among other purposes, this type of abstinence was a way for Samuel to show to the people around him that he was different from them and that he was in special service to God. It was a public way of making a spiritual statement. We find in the prophecy of the birth of John the Baptist (Luke 1:15), and the description of his clothing (Matt. 3:4), that he too adopted an appearance and conduct which told people that he was in special service to God. People should be able to look at us and realize that we are peculiar—different from the rest—because we are in special service to God.

Consider the use of the word "peculiar" in the King James version. "The Lord hath chosen thee to be a peculiar people unto himself" (Deut. 14:2). The church is a "peculiar people, zealous of good works" (Titus 2:14). Although the word here means "special" and not "strange," think of the implications of the later. Samuel probably was a little strange, different from everyone else. John the Baptist certain was. They conducted themselves, and maintained an appearance, which was strange, different. It was obvious to everyone that they were in special service to God.

Samuel was born and, probably within the second year (1 Sam. 1:24), was taken to live with Eli in the Temple. Yet every year his mother returned with a new cloak for the growing boy (2:19). In discussing Moses we pointed out the importance of parental contact in a child's early years. The teaching in one's youth is not easily forgotten. Samuel serves as a reminder of this truth.

But things were not well in Shiloh. On the other end of the spectrum from Hannah were Eli's sons, wicked men who "had no regard for the Lord" (2:12). They took meat from sacrifices that belonged to the Lord and to the offerer (1 Sam. 2:13-16; see Lev. 7:30-34). They were also sleeping with the women who worked in the Temple (1 Sam. 2:22). Eli made a feeble attempt to stop them but it did no good (2:23-25). (In contrast to them, the author twice points out that Samuel was growing in favor with the Lord and with men, 2:21,26.)

Sin cannot go unpunished. Eli's sons had laughed in the face of God and had to pay the price. A "man of God" told Eli that both his sons would die on the same day (2:27-36). The Israelites fought the Philistines and the sons were killed; and when Eli heard the news he fell over backward, broke his neck, and died (4:1-18).

Let's talk about accountability. Although it was

Eli's sons who were sinning, see what the man of God said. "This is what the Lord says: . . . Why do you [Eli] scorn my sacrifice and offering . . . ? Why do you honor your sons more than me by fattening yourselves on the choice parts of every offering made by my people Israel? . . . The time is coming when I will cut short your strength and the strength of your father's house, so that there will not be an old man in your family line . . . . Every one of you that I do not cut off from my altar will be spared only to blind your eyes with tears and to grieve your heart, and all your descendants will die in the prime of life" (2:27,29,31,33). Eli was responsible for not stopping his sons.

There certainly is a point at which a parent is no longer responsible for the actions of the children. But Eli was in a position to do something about the situation and he was held accountable for not doing so (3:13). Notice too that Eli's descendants paid the price for his lack of responsibility. The sins of the fathers most certainly are visited upon the children.

Before we are told that Eli died, we read the story of Samuel's call by God. Three times God audibly called the young boy, until finally Eli figured out what was happening and told Samuel to answer, "Speak, Lord, for your servant is listening" (3:9). God told Samuel that Eli's punishment would come soon.

Times change. In those days God spoke audibly, appeared in human form, and even argued with people (see, for example, Exod. 3:1-14). Today, we can hear His voice every day in the words of Scripture. And we can hear Him speaking, although not normally audibly, through the ministry of His Holy Spirit. Have you ever been studying a scriptural passage that makes absolutely no sense, then all of a sudden, like a flash, you know what it means? This is what the doctrine of illumination is all about. It is the Holy Spirit making clear the teaching of Scripture. The "flash" you experienced was not audible but it was just as clear and understandable as if you actually heard words. Times change. Ways of doing things change, but He is still the one and same Lord, living in communion with His creation. It is just that now Scripture and the Holy Spirit are His usual means of communication.

Eli died. The ark which had been captured in battle was returned, and Samuel became judge over all Israel (1 Sam. 3:19–7:1). About twenty years later the Philistines attacked Israel, and the Israelites came to Samuel saying, "Do not stop crying out to the Lord our God for us, that he may rescue us from the hand of the Philistines" (7:8). Samuel continued to pray to God and the Philistines were defeated.

Prayer continued to be an essential part of Samuel's life. When Israel asked for a king, Samuel prayed for direction (8:6). When God expressed His displeasure with Saul, Samuel spent the entire night in prayer (15:11). Samuel, like his mother, knew the value of constant, intense prayer.

When Samuel was old he appointed his sons to judge Israel. But as was the case with Eli, Samuel's sons were also wicked men, dishonest, and politically corrupt.

We can all learn from Samuel's mistake. Unfortunately, he did not learn from Eli's.

Samuel's most important contribution came at the end of his life. Israel was in the process of becoming a nation. It was a transitional period in which instability ruled: there was fighting on the borders and within; the people had to contend with a highly erratic king, yet, in the midst of it all stood Samuel, a stable rock, maintaining balance in a slippery age.

Israel wanted a king. Samuel's sons were worthless judges, and the nation wanted to be like other nations. Their sin was not in wanting a king—this was part of God's future plans for the nation; for how can you have a nation without a king? (David certainly was in God's will.) Their sin was in wanting it "Now!" contrary to God's will.

What is the danger of not submitting to the will of God? God just might give you what you want. Strange sounding, but true. Israel rejected God as their king (1 Sam. 8:7) because they wanted an earthly king, and "so in my anger I [God] gave you a king" (Hos. 13:11). They insisted on a king, got Saul, and paid a price.

The danger of fighting against the will of God is that He might give you what you want. The irony, of course, is that what we think we want and what is really good for us are often two different things. Israel wanted a king, and they got Saul.

Samuel warned the people about the problems of a king, but stories of inscription and taxation would not discourage them. They wanted to be like the other nations (1 Sam. 8:20). They had not yet learned they were to be a peculiar people. So, in a three-fold manner Saul became Israel's first king. He was anointed by Samuel (9:1-10), was presented to the people (10:17-27), and proved himself in battle against the Ammonites (chap. 11).

Samuel was a confronter. He confronted the entire nation with their sin of requesting a king (12:7-13). He confronted Saul when he had sacrificed improperly before fighting the Philistines (13:11-14). He confronted Saul again when he did not destroy all the animals captured from the Amalekites; Saul was therefore rejected as king by God (15:12-31).

Confronting is not fun. There is something inside most of us that winces when we are faced with the necessity to confront. But Samuel helps us here. Sin is sin. It is repulsive and must be dealt with. If not, it will grow like a cancer until it has destroyed the whole organism.

Take, for example, your church. Are there any members who are living in constant sin? Hear the word of the Lord. "You must not associate with anyone who calls himself a brother but is sexually immoral or greedy, an idolator or a slanderer, a drunkard or a swindler. With such a man do not even eat" (1 Cor. 5:11). We can ignore this command—and it is a command—and pay the price, or we can respect the authority of Scripture and be obedient.

The church is rapidly becoming non-confrontist. Some would say, the church is for "sick" people (Mark 2:17); we can't excommunicate the very people we are trying to help." Two issues are at stake here. The first is the authority of Scripture. Do we listen to human arguments or to the words of God? The second is the problem of confronting. Confronting makes us uncomfortable. We do not want to be unpopular by being judgmental. We are no longer repulsed by sin. But Scripture does not give us this option. Jesus confronted sin. Samuel confronted sin. Will you?

Samuel teaches us something else about confronting. Samuel never saw Saul after confronting him the final time, but he did mourn for Saul (1 Sam. 15:35). Samuel did not haughtily condemn Saul. He spoke forcibly and firmly as a spokesman for God; yet down deep he was mourning. Likewise, when we confront, our attitude must be one of sorrow, yet still recognizing that the task must be done. They who confront vindictively, pridefully, need to check out the log in their eye first before removing the speck in another's (see Matt. 7:1-5).

We do not hear much about Samuel after this. David fled to Samuel while Saul was pursuing him (1 Sam. 19:18-24). We are told that when he died, "all Israel assembled and mourned for him" (25:1). The final mention of Samuel is when Saul conjures his spirit up from the dead (28:1-19).

What can be said about Samuel? He came from a devout home and was raised in the service of God. He provided stability in a volatile time as Israel evolved into an organized nation. Through Samuel God appointed, strengthened, and rejected the first king. And through it all Samuel stood, probably lonely, isolated, but firmly—God's man in a transitional time.

Discussion Questions

1. Critique your prayer life. How badly do you really want the things for which you pray? Do you pray constantly (see Luke 18:1-8)? Do you pray fervently?

2. Can people tell that you are a Christian just by looking? What practical steps can you take to make your spiritual commitment more obvious? Give examples of how you can take this principle too far.

3. Think up three situations in which parents are accountable for the actions of their children. Think up three in which parents are not.

4. How has God spoken very clearly to you in Bible study and prayer?

5. Have you ever insisted on your way contrary to the wishes of God? What happened?

6. Are you a confronter? What is it inside you that makes it especially hard to confront? Share an example of how you should confront and how you should not.

7. Has God ever placed you in a pivotal position at a very important time? What was it and how did it go? Would Samuel have been proud?

Note
1. William S. LaSor, *Great Personalities of the Old Testament* (Old Tappan, NJ: Fleming H. Revell Co., 1959).

Chapter 8

David:
Dedication to the Lord

Of all the Old Testament figures, David is by far the best known. His life and writings have taught and inspired people down through the centuries. Much has been written about him, but there is always more to learn. That is the beauty of Scripture.

The story of David's life can be divided into three parts. The first is his youth in which he fought Goliath and served in Saul's court. The second is his time as a political fugitive, running from Saul and living among the Philistines. The third is his return to Israel and the establishment of his kingdom.

We first read of David in the book of Ruth when we find that Ruth was his great grandmother (Ruth 4:21). When discussing her life we said that God was the main Actor in the story, active in the little, mundane affairs of life. And yet out of these "little" things came King David who brought God's promise that Abraham's descendants would be a nation to fulfillment (Gen. 12:2).

David's life story begins in 1 Samuel 13. Saul sinned by sacrificing improperly before a battle. The prophet Samuel confronted him with the grim news that his dynasty would be destroyed, for "the Lord has sought out a man after his own heart and appointed him leader of his people" (13:14). Samuel subsequently traveled to Bethlehem and anointed David as king (16:1-13).

But this anointing was different from Saul's anointing. Saul was very tall and probably quite good looking (9:2; 10:24)—every inch a king. When Samuel went to Bethlehem he thought at first that Eliab, one of David's older brothers, was to be king because of his appearance (16:6). But "the Lord does not look at the things man looks at. Man looks at the outward appearance, but the Lord looks at the heart" (16:7). Unlike man, God raises up individuals not on the basis of outward appearances but on inward realities. Saul and Eliab may have looked regal but that did not mean that they were fit to serve. David, on the other hand, had a kingly heart.

Unfortunately, much of our personal evaluation of friends and acquaintances is based on outward appearances and not on true inner worth. We all know of times when our standard of judgment, like Samuel's, has been wrong.

This is not to say that David was not good looking. He was a "ruddy" and handsome boy, the youngest of eight brothers (16:11-12). LaSor says that, traditionally, "ruddy" means blue-eyed, fair complected with blonde or reddish hair. But what is more important is that David had a heart for God.

From the day of his anointing "the Spirit of the Lord came upon David in power" (16:13). This may not seem that unusual to us, but it is almost unique in the Old Testament. The working of the Holy Spirit is one of the main differences between the New and Old Testaments. Since Pentecost, believers are in continual possession of the Holy Spirit; this is the mark of a Christian (Rom. 8:9). But in the Old Testament one generally received the Spirit as a temporary empowering for a specific task. The judges of Israel are good examples of this. The Spirit of the Lord came upon Othniel (Judg. 3:10), upon Gideon (6:34), upon Jephthah (11:29), and each went to war. The Spirit of the Lord came upon Samson three times, enabling him to kill a lion (14:6), kill thirty Philistines (14:19), and to break his own bonds (15:14). The Spirit of the Lord also came upon Saul; he prophesied (1 Sam. 10:6,10; 19:23) and went to war (11:6). But the Spirit of the Lord was to reside on David always. God looked upon David's heart and empowered him in a very special way to carry out his God-given task.

When God rejected Saul and left him, a tormenting evil spirit came upon him. Only music could calm him during these "fits," so he summoned David who not only played the lyre but played it well.

David was a brave man, a warrior, and very articulate (16:18). He was one of those people who could do almost everything. And when he did something, he did it well (18:5).

The writer of Ecclesiastes instructs, "Whatever your hand finds to do, do it with all your might, for in the grave, where you are going, there is neither

working nor planning nor knowledge nor wisdom"
(Eccles. 9:10). A thousand years after David, the
Apostle Paul told slaves to "Serve wholeheartedly,
as if you were serving the Lord, not men" (Eph.
6:7). If something is worth doing, it is worth doing
well, with all your energy.

Why go to college and not give it your best? Why
start a career and only do the minimum? Why
start a family, knowing all along you do not have
enough time to give to them? It is a choice. Medi-
ocrity is a habit that can be broken. This is not a
call for unbridled workaholism. It is a plea for
responsible stewardship of God's gifts. God has
given us a life; we are responsible for how we use
it. Time is not ours to squander.

The movie *Chariots of Fire* was a character
study of two runners preparing for the Olympic
games. One ran for his own glory; the other ran for
the Lord. In fact, his running was so much for the
Lord's glory that he would not run in his main
event because it was held on Sunday. Surely many
came away from the movie with a new resolve to
pursue excellence. When David did something, he
did it well.

Israel and the Philistines were at war again (1
Sam. 17). But this time the enemy had a nine-foot
giant, Goliath, who came up with a "brilliant"
idea. Instead of the two armies fighting, he sug-
gested that the Israelites pick a champion to
oppose him, and the country of the loser would
serve the other. Goliath taunted the Israelites this
way for forty days, and no one was found to challenge him.

David had left his flocks to bring food to his
brothers in the army. When he heard Goliath's

challenge he asked, "Who is this uncircumcised Philistine that he should defy the armies of the living God?" (17:26). When no one else would, David offered to fight. The passage provides an interesting sidelight into David's family life. David's older brother heard his offer, and accused him of being conceited, wicked, and coming only to watch the battle. David replied with the words so often heard in homes today: "I can't even say anything without getting yelled at"—a slight paraphrase of 1 Samuel 17:29.

Because of his offer, David was taken to Saul who apparently did not remember who the boy was, probably because of his unstable mental condition. David pointed out that he had already killed a lion and a bear, and the God who had helped him then would help him now. He refused any armor—what does a shepherd know about this type of equipment—found five stones polished smooth by a stream, and faced Goliath with this challenge: "You come against me with sword and spear and javelin, but I come against you in the name of the Lord Almighty, the God of the armies of Israel, whom you have defied. This day the Lord will hand you over to me, and I'll strike you down and cut off your head. Today I will give the carcasses of the Philistine army to the birds of the air and the beasts of the earth, and the whole world will know that there is a God in Israel. All those gathered here will know that it is not by sword or spear that the Lord saves; for the battle is the Lord's, and he will give all of you into our hands" (1 Sam. 17:45-47).

A beautiful statement of faith. Goliath had not so much insulted the Israelites as he had insulted their God, and his punishment will come not from man but from God. As Joshua had learned, David knew: victory is from the Lord. The victor is the one who relies on God. As the defeat of Jericho had illustrated, now it would be obvious to all that God would fight the battle and kill the infidel (17:46).

David's sling was a small, round piece of leather or fabric with two strings, each about one and a half feet long, attached to either side; the rock fit in the round part. The sling was swung around and around and when one of the strings was released the centrifugal force would send the rock flying. David used his sling skillfully and the rock stunned Goliath. David ran and got the giant's sword, killed him, and then cut off his head (17:49-51). After the battle Saul kept David at the court.

David's life in Saul's service was varied. He met Jonathan, Saul's son, and they became as close as two friends can become (1 Sam. 18:1-4; 19:1; 20:17,41). David proved himself to be very successful in battle (18:5,14,30), so much so that Saul became jealous. Not only did he try to kill David twice himself (18:11; 19:10) but he even tried to arrange his death by the hands of the Philistines (18:17,25) and others (19:11). However, with the help of Jonathan, David escaped.

This exile marks the second part of David's life. At first he fled to a Philistine city, but there too he was in danger. So he pretended to be insane and escaped (21:10-15). He went to the cave of Adullam where he was joined by Israelites who were in debt or were discontented.

What follows is a cat-and-mouse game, with

Saul pursuing and David always staying one step ahead. It must have been frustrating for David to flee from a king to whom he was still loyal. Despite such frustrations, David's trust in the Lord continued to grow. He relied on God's direction through use of the ephod (1 Sam. 23:2-4,9-12; 30:7). Psalm 57—its heading dates the psalm during this time in David's life—also witnesses to that faith. Perhaps this trust in God is most clearly seen when David twice refused ripe opportunities to kill Saul (chaps. 24,26). Saul was still the king, the Lord's anointed, and David would not harm him (24:6,10; 26:9-11; see also 2 Sam. 1:11-16,19-27).

The only situation in which David's faith may have wavered occurred when he lived with the Philistines (1 Sam. 27) and was willing to fight with them against Israel (chap. 28). David may have gotten tired of being chased and gave up (27:1). As was the case with Abraham, the Bible paints a very human, honest portrait of David. It is not afraid to show the bad with the good. (But we should be a bit hesitant to read too much between the lines. We know that previous to this, David had been raiding the enemies of Israel but telling the Philistines that he was attacking Israel [1 Sam. 27:8-12]. He may have had something else up his sleeve here.)

There is today, and perhaps always has been, the sad misconception that the truly strong person relies on himself and on no one else. "I can do it on my own!" "I am my own man." "God helps those who help themselves." This attitude strikes at the heart of the Christian faith and comes from a complete misunderstanding of the Christian's relation to God and to those around them. It is a misunderstanding especially prevalent among those of us who have an insatiable desire to be independent. Benjamin Franklin may have thought that God helps those who help themselves, but David certainly did not.

As a youth David stood before a giant with only a sling, and taunted him. He led a ferocious band of marauders. He knit a nation together against insurmountable odds. Yet, the Bible says that he drew his strength not from himself but from God. When David and his men returned to their home at Ziklag they found the Amalekites had raided the city and taken their wives and children captive. His own men were thinking of stoning David, "but David found strength in the Lord his God" (1 Sam. 30:6). Earlier, while he was fleeing from Saul, David was visited by Jonathan at Horesh and "found strength in God" (23:16). David was a powerful man in his own right, yet he needed help and encouragement from his friends and his God.

God has made us social and dependent creatures who do not have the strength within ourselves to run the race. We must recognize our need for others, especially to draw strength from the Source of all strength.

Saul killed himself after being defeated by the Philistines. David then was anointed king of southern Israel in Hebron. Abner, the commander of Saul's army, kept power in the north for several years. But eventually he gave the north over to David who then ruled the nation as a whole. This began the third stage of his life.

David was a shrewd politician. He wept bitterly

over Abner's death so that all Israel knew he had no part in the murder (2 Sam. 3:37). The nation also surely heard of David's remorse at Saul's death. David killed the men who had killed Saul's son Ishbosheth (4:12), and he treated Jonathan's son Mephibosheth graciously (9:6-7). Surely there were other factors behind his actions, but the political ramifications were important. The nation was split in two: Judah to the south was pro-David; Israel to the north was pro-Saul. David's actions cemented the divided kingdom together.

The choice of Jerusalem as the capitol was a shrewd one. Up to this point the city was controlled by the Jebusites, and belonged neither to the north nor the south. It was neutral ground politically, very much like the United States capitol in Washington, D.C., does not belong to a specific state but is controlled by the country as a whole. David brought the ark to Jerusalem, making the city both the political and religious center of the nation (chap. 6). So at thirty David was ruler of a united kingdom (2 Sam. 5:1-5). He eventually defeated the Philistines and other neighboring nations, and brought peace and prosperity to the land.

We know well of his sin with Bathsheba. It illustrates another important fact about David. David felt the pangs of sin deeply and was earnest in his repentance. Because God looks on the intentions of the heart, David could be called "a man after his own heart" (1 Sam. 13:14). God is concerned more with who we are than with what we do.

So David died, having ruled Judah seven and a half years, and the united kingdom thirty-three

years. Politically he was a wise and powerful war-
rior-king. As a poet and musician he was without
equal. But perhaps above all else, we see a man
fully dedicated to the Lord, relying on Him for
strength and victory (see 1 Sam. 18:14; 30:23; 2
Sam. 2:1; 4:9; see also many of his psalms). We see
a man whose heart was centered in a vital, living
relationship with his God.

Discussion Questions

1. How do you tend to judge people? When has
your surface judgment been completely wrong?

2. To what degree of excellence do you strive?
When was the last time you did something halfway
and it backfired? At what point does the pursuit of
excellence become a license for workaholism?

3. When Goliath insulted the armies of Israel
he was insulting their God. How does this happen
today? When it happens to you, what do you do?

4. Have you ever tried to be loyal to someone
who was trying to harm you? What happened?

5. How do you answer someone who says that
"God helps those who help themselves"? In what
sense is this saying true, and in what sense false?

6. Have you ever, like Jonathan, helped someone find strength in the Lord? How does that compare with trying to do it your own way?

7. Are you seeking God's own heart? Or are
you unable to repent?

Chapter 9

Elijah: A Brutal Man for Brutal Times

The years of David's reign were the Golden Years of Israel. The borders were expanded and commerce flourished. Under Solomon the Temple was built, and prosperity increased. But when Solomon grew old, problems came. In his youth, he had gone against the commands of the Lord and had married women from the neighboring countries—700 wives and 300 concubines. When he got old, the influence of these women turned him away from the true God and he worshiped the gods of their native lands (1 Kings 11:1-8).

Joshua had warned the nation not to intermarry, especially with the Canaanites, but they disobeyed. When Solomon lost the strength and commitment of his youth, he disobeyed, and was led into false worship.

A similar situation led Paul to write "Do not be yoked together with unbelievers" (2 Cor. 6:14; see also 1 Cor. 7:39). The metaphor here pictures two people bound closely together, like two oxen joined with a large wooden yoke.

But what kind of situation can be considered a "yoking"? Certainly marriage is one, but the principle stated by Paul, and illustrated here by Israel is not one pertaining solely to marriage. Christians and non-Christians do not belong together in intimate relationships. We are all social creatures; we are influenced by those around us. It is total foolishness to think that associates, friends, and spouse do not have an influence.

Our churches are filled with people whose lives speak to this principle: men and women who have ignored this simple truth from Scripture. They have paid the price and now bear the pain. Yet there is hope. Imagine the ministry these broken people could now have with the youth in our churches: "Look at my life; look at what happened to Israel. Listen and be obedient to the words of the law."

When Solomon sinned, God raised up enemies and prophesied that Solomon's son would lose all of the kingdom except the southern tribe of Judah. When his son Rehoboam came to power, the elder advisors said he should lighten the taxation while the younger advisors encouraged him to increase them. Unfortunately, Rehoboam listened to the younger, and the northern ten tribes seceded under the leadership of Jeroboam (1 Kings 12:1-24). At this point the name "Israel" came to refer to the northern kingdom, and "Judah" to the southern.

In order to secure his own kingdom, Jeroboam set up two altars on the southern and northern borders of Israel, at Bethel and Dan. Jerusalem was in Judah, and Jeroboam was afraid that if his people went to Jerusalem to worship, they would eventually turn against him. He also built places for sacrifice throughout the land, and appointed priests (1 Kings 12:25-33). This was a politically wise move, but spelled the eventual death of the northern kingdom. It completed the division between the north and the south, and opened the floodgate for pagan religions to defile Israel.

The southern kingdom had its problems. Rehoboam fluctuated in his obedience to God. His son Abijah was even worse. But Abijah's son Asa was a good king. Asa removed pagan religious practices, and even deposed his grandmother Maacah who worshiped Asherah. Asa ruled for forty-one years (15:9-24).

Things in the northern kingdom were much worse. Jeroboam continued to be a wicked king; his son Nadab who ruled after him was killed by Baasha. When Baasha died, his son Elah ruled two years, and Zimri killed him. The army mutinied and made Omri king; he ruled twelve years, died, and his son Ahab began to rule. Seven kings in thirty-six years. And the rule of each was an abomination to the Lord (chaps. 15–16).

Yet, no matter how abysmal the others were, Ahab was the worst of all (21:25-26). He married Jezebel, the daughter of the king of Phoenicia. As was the custom, she brought the worship of her gods, Baal and Asherah, to Israel. Ahab built a temple in Samaria, appointed and paid for 450 priests for Baal and 400 prophets for Asherah (1 Kings 16:31-33; 18:19). He even sacrificed two of his sons (16:34) in direct disobedience to God's law (Lev. 18:21; 20:1-5).

Ahab represents the epitome of religious syncretism in Israel, the culmination of a process that began hundreds of years earlier. To fully understand this process we need to go back to Joshua, and perhaps even further to Abraham. Why did God choose Canaan of all places to send Abraham? Why not to some other more promising area? Someone once said that Moses wandered forty years in the wilderness only to find the one country which did not have oil. Although this may be true, Israel's location in the ancient world was strategic. To the south was Egypt, one of the most important of all ancient empires and the breadbasket of the ancient world. To the north lay the great empires of Assyria, Babylonia, Persia, Rome, and others. To the west was the sea, and to the east a great desert. The only way to get to Egypt on foot was to go through Canaan, the crossroads of the ancient world. It was the perfect headquarters for the spread of God's truth to the world through merchants, sailors, armies, and travelers. Perhaps this accounts for its position as the Promised Land.

The problem of syncretism arose when Joshua was not fully obedient to God's commands. He was commanded to conquer all the land and to kill all the people. Instead, he conquered only most of the hill country and killed only some of the people. The western part of Canaan, a flat, fertile plain, was inhabited by the Philistines in the south and the Phoenecians in the north. Moving inland, the plain is met by a low range of hills called the *Shephelah*. East of the Shephelah are the higher Judean mountains, and east of these mountains lies the Jordan. Joshua conquered most of the high ground, some of the Shephelah, but none of the plain. Consequently the nation of Israel had to deal with the Gibeonites (Josh. 9:3-27), Jebusites (15:63), Canaanites (16:10; 17:12-13,16-18), and others (11:22; 13:13; 23:4-5). Joshua may have expected those who followed him to finish the conquest after his death (23:4-5). But whoever be at fault, the other nations were not destroyed.

Failure to conquer the plain was an especially regretful error. Not only were the Philistines a continual thorn in Israel's side, but the plain was the most traveled part of the region. If Israel had controlled it, and if the faith had remained pure, Israel's influence on the ancient world would have been decidedly strengthened.

The price paid for partial obedience is a bitter pill to swallow. The land was not conquered; Israel never reached its full potential in the ancient world. And despite Joshua's command (Josh. 23:6-13), Israel mixed freely and even intermarried with other nations. The religion became polluted, a pollution which would build to a climax at the time of Elijah.

Combined with the influence of other nations on Israel's religion, was the economic and social condition of the time. Although Omri was a wicked king, he was successful in providing economic prosperity, especially evidenced by his building program. But while the rich were getting richer, the poor were getting poorer, so poor that some even had to sell themselves as slaves (see 2 Kings 4:1). Some scholars suspect that the drought caused by Elijah's prayer (1 Kings 17–18) forced smaller farmers to sell their land to larger farms.[1]

North and south were continually fighting. In

Israel there was political instability, religious syncretism, and economic depravity. To make mat-
ters worse, Ahab married the foreign Jezebel. She
"was a strong-minded woman filled with an almost
missionary zeal for her god and no doubt con-
temptuous of the cultural backwardness and aus-
tere religion of her adopted land, [who] apparently
sought to make the cult of Ba'al the official religion of the court"² (see, for example, 1 Kings
18:13). It was a brutal time.

Israel paid the price for mixing with the
Canaanites, and into their unstable and wicked
situation God sent Elijah, a prophet, to be His
mouthpiece. Until Elijah's time, prophets were
basically advisors to the king, helping him rule by
God's direction and lending support to kingdom
policies. But under Ahab, the kingdom was in
deep trouble; Elijah's message was not one of cor-
rection and hope but of doom.

Elijah was not a man to be trifled with. A loner,
a nomad of the wilderness, he would appear, then
disappear to be found somewhere else (1 Kings
18:12). His appearance was ragged, his clothing
rough (2 Kings 1:8). He spoke a harsh and vengeful message, with the energy and authority
expected of a prophet of God. Elijah was hated
fiercely by Ahab (1 Kings 18:10), who called the
prophet "troubler of Israel" (18:17) and "my
enemy" (21:20). Elijah was a brutal man, but these
were brutal times.

We first encounter Elijah in 1 Kings 17, where
he told Ahab that there would be no rain—not
even any dew—for several years (v. 1). Following
his pronouncement he returned to the land east of
the Jordan where ravens brought him food. When

the water there dried up, he lived with a widow and her son in Zarephath, a Phoenecian city eight miles south of Sidon. There God continually replenished the jar of flour and the jug of oil, and Elijah raised her dead son.

After three years of drought, Elijah returned to Israel. He found Ahab and challenged him to a contest between Baal and the true God. When the people came from all over the northern kingdom to watch, Elijah met them with this challenge: "How long will you waver between two opinions? If the Lord is God, follow him; but if Baal is God, follow him" (1 Kings 18:21). In other words, "Fish or cut bait!" Still, the people said nothing. The prophets of Baal built an altar, sacrificed a bull, and called upon Baal to light the fire. They danced around the altar from morning until noon, but nothing happened.

Elijah began to taunt them. "Maybe he is deep in thought, or going to the bathroom, or traveling. Maybe he is sleeping; shout louder." (The Hebrew is idiomatic for "going to the bathroom"—18:27. The *NIV* softens it by translating it as "he is . . . busy.") So Elijah built an altar, sacrificed a bull, and poured so much water over it that the trench surrounding the altar was filled. The prophet prayed and God sent fire down and consumed not only the sacrifice and wood, but also the stones of the altar, the dirt, and the water. The prophets of Baal were killed, and rain returned to the land.

God is often described as a "jealous" God; He is possessive. He does not want to share us with anything or with anyone else. The Israelites watching this spectacle had rejected God for Baal, and Baal could not even light a fire. Instead, the awesome power of the God they had rejected descended and disintegrated the very altar itself in a flash of fire. Confronted with power of this magnitude, knowing that God had demanded their complete and total allegiance, these people must have experienced a righteous fear unlike anything before. The message for us remains the same: "Fish or cut bait." He will not share you with the world and its gods.

When Jezebel heard that her prophets were killed and her god ridiculed, she threatened to kill Elijah. This great prophet, who had called down fire from heaven and rebuked kings, ran, hid, and prayed that God would take his life (1 Kings 19:1-5). Weakness can follow closely on the heels of strength; a time of peace does not necessarily follow a time of victory.

An angel strengthened Elijah, and he traveled south to a mountain in Sinai called *Horeb*, the same mountain where Moses had received the Ten Commandments. Elijah was tired, discouraged, and afraid. He had tried his best, but to no avail. He was the only faithful one left—so he thought (19:9-10).

We have all felt like this. After trying our best we discover it wasn't good enough. Our efforts were ignored, and even opposed. Now we feel all alone, with no one on our side. Sound familiar? Hear joyfully the word of the Lord.

Elijah went to the mouth of the cave, and the Lord passed by. He spoke not in the great wind that rushed by nor in the earthquake or fire. God spoke to Elijah in a "gentle whisper," a still small voice (19:12). Most of us know people who claim that God has spoken to them in a great and mighty way. They may be right, but that type of experience is certainly not normative. We need not feel neglected or belittled if God has not spoken to us in this way. Usually when God speaks, it is with the gentle whisper of a father calming his young child.

God told Elijah that he was not alone, for God had reserved "seven thousand in Israel—all whose knees have not bowed down to Baal and all whose mouths have not kissed him" (1 Kings 19:18). Although all of Abraham's descendants were not saved, there were a few, a "remnant," who had been faithful to God.

The prophet Isaiah continually proclaimed that only a remnant of the people would return from captivity (Isa. 10:20-23; see also Rom. 9:27-28). In Paul's day, a remnant remained (Rom. 11:5). Salvation is not automatically given to all of Abraham's descendants; salvation is a gift of grace to the few who are faithful (Rom. 11:6). God is faithful to His promises. The world will be blessed because a remnant of Abraham's descendants were faithful to God, and to them God will graciously give the gift of salvation.

So Elijah returned to Israel. Eventually, Ahab died and his son Ahaziah ruled in his place. But he, like his father, was wicked. After two years, Ahaziah asked the god of Ekron if he would recover from an injury. Because he did not inquire of the true God, Elijah pronounced his doom, and Ahaziah died.

The story of Elijah's life concludes with his rapture into heaven in a fiery chariot and a whirlwind. Like Enoch before him, Elijah did not have to taste death.

Elijah is mentioned in two other significant places in Scripture. The final prophecy in the Old Testament said that Elijah would come back to earth in order to prepare the people for the coming of God's kingdom (Mal. 4:5-6). This prophecy was, of course, fulfilled by John the Baptist, although he was not Elijah reincarnated in the flesh (John 1:21). He was an Elijah-type person, in dress (Matt. 3:4) and in force of message, who prepared Israel for the coming of Christ (Matt. 3:1-3).

Scripture's final mention of Elijah is on the Mount of Transfiguration with Moses and Jesus (Luke 9:28-31). Here these representatives of the Law and the Prophets witnessed to the continual rejection of God's messengers by the people of Israel, and to Christ's death which was necessary to restore mankind to fellowship with God. Israel had been unfaithful to God from the very beginning. Yet God remained faithful to His promises to Abraham, and to His promise that some day the seed of the woman would crush the serpent's head.

Discussion Questions

1. The picture we get of the northern kingdom shows that a nation's worth is measured by its commitment to God. Can you see any resemblance between Israel and your nation?

2. God placed Israel in a strategic location. Has He placed you where your Christian witness can be especially effective?

3. Are you maintaining the purity of your faith in this non-Christian world? What sort of things

do you find especially destructive to your walk with the Lord?

4. Are you yoked with unbelievers? Give three types of relationships which are a "yoking."

5. What are two practical ways of avoiding a yoking with nonbelievers? Think of three different situations in which a Christian is improperly yoked, and what your advice would be.

6. What has happened in your life that illustrates the truth that God is a jealous God?

7. How does God speak to you?

Notes
1. John Bright, *A History of Israel* (Philadelphia: Westminster Press, 1974), p. 240 f.
2. Ibid., p. 241.

Chapter 10

Isaiah:
Judgment and Hope

The New Testament refers to the writings of Isaiah at least sixty-six times, more than any other Old Testament book except the Psalms. Isaiah's influence is not bound in time; his lessons are continually applicable.

Ever since the northern kingdom of Israel had separated from Judah to the south, the southern kingdom had been on a spiritual roller coaster. Good kings were followed by bad kings; bad kings were followed by mediocre ones. Isaiah, whose name means "the Lord saves," was a prophet to Judah at a crucial point on this roller coaster, when salvation was most desperately needed.

We know very little about the prophet himself; what can be known must be gleaned from his writings and from his historical situation.

Asa was a righteous king who instituted religious reform and enjoyed a military peace for most of his forty-one year reign. He was succeeded by his son Jehoshaphat, who also enjoyed a long reign of relative peace and prosperity.

Unfortunately, upon his death and his son Jehoram's rise to power, things became intolerable. Jehoram married Athaliah, a daughter of Ahab, Israel's wicked king. It was partially through her influence that Jehoram reinstituted pagan religious practices and even killed his six brothers to secure the throne. After he had reigned eight years, the Philistines attacked his house and took captive all but his wife Athaliah and son Ahaziah (2 Kings 8:16-24).

Ahaziah ruled for less than a year before he was killed in battle (8:25–9:29). Athaliah took the throne, continued to enforce Baal worship, and killed all of the royal family except Ahaziah's young son Joash, who was hidden by his aunt.

When Joash was seven, through the trickery of the priest, Jehoiada, Joash was crowned and Athaliah killed. During his forty-year reign, Joash instituted sweeping reforms. The temple of Baal was destroyed, although some of the high places of worship remained. The Solomonic Temple was repaired and sacrifices begun (11:4–12:8). However, when Jehoiada the priest died, the officials of Judah persuaded Joash to return to Baal worship. The next year Jerusalem was invaded, and Joash was wounded. Some of his officials killed him because he had killed the son of Jehoiada who had prophesied against him (2 Chron. 24:17-25).

Joash's son Amaziah assumed the throne in 796 B.C. and ruled for twenty-nine years. As many of his predecessors before him had done, Amaziah followed the Lord, "but not wholeheartedly" (2 Chron. 25:2). He challenged Israel to battle, and was soundly defeated. Jerusalem's walls were partially destroyed, its treasures plundered, and Amaziah taken captive. When Amaziah was taken captive around 790 B.C., his sixteen-year-old son Uzziah (who was also called Azariah) became co-regent and ruled for fifty-two years (2 Kings 14; 2 Chron. 25).

Judah was at its lowest point. They had been totally defeated, and not until his father was released some years later could Uzziah begin rebuilding the nation. During this time Isaiah was a scribe in the royal court.

Isaiah was born in the middle of the 700s. His father Amoz was, according to tradition, the brother of King Amaziah, Uzziah's father. If this tradition is correct, Isaiah was of royal blood and a cousin to King Uzziah.

As a scribe Isaiah's job was to keep an historical record of the times. This gave him great exposure to the political happenings of the court, and secured for him an excellent education. His extensive vocabulary and command of the language speaks to this, as any student of Hebrew is painfully aware. He had a poetic ability to paint word pictures with beautiful metaphors, showing a real sensitivity to the language.

Uzziah expanded Judah's boundaries considerably and prosperity increased. In fact the nation's prosperity became greater than at any time previous except for that of David and Solomon.

For the most part Uzziah did what was right in the eyes of the Lord, but he did not remove all the high places of idol worship. In his pride he offered incense in the Temple, a duty belonging solely to the priest. He was struck with leprosy and lived the rest of his life in seclusion (2 Kings 15:1-7; 2 Chron. 26). His son Jotham was made co-regent, and king at Uzziah's death in 740 B.C.

When Uzziah died, Isaiah was called by God to be a prophet to the southern kingdom. His life as a scribe and his descent from royal blood gained him easy access to the court and the priesthood. He spoke fearlessly the words of God. He had the gift of faith, and never seemed to waver in his commitment. As Youngblood says, "So great a man was Isaiah that it is difficult to exaggerate when describing him."[1]

But problems were rising in the north. The Assyrian Tiglath-pileser III conquered the Babylonians, and in 743 B.C. forced Israel to pay a very large tribute. Although his army did not go as far south as Judah, there was a national dread of the superpower. King Jotham was anti-Assyrian, so the political opposition forced his son Ahaz who was pro-Assyrian into a co-regency. When Jotham died in 732 B.C., Ahaz assumed full power.

Ahaz's sixteen-year rule was a difficult time (2 Kings 16; 2 Chron. 28). He had established ties with the Assyrians while Israel and Syria had decided to resist. When Syria attacked Judah, Ahaz did not know what to do. Isaiah advised him that if he would have faith in God he would have nothing to fear (Isa. 7:1-9). Isaiah told Ahaz to ask for a sign from God that this would be, but Ahaz refused, not out of piety or great faith, but because he had already rejected the worship of the true God. He was worshiping regularly at the pagan high places and had even sacrificed his sons to Molech at Ben Hinnom. (Ben Hinnom is synonymous with Gehenna, the valley forming the west side of Jerusalem.) Because of Ahaz's sin, the valley eventually became ceremonially unclean and suitable only for a trash dump. The continual fires and stench arising from it formed the perfect basis for Jesus' illustration of hell in His teachings.

Despite Ahaz's unbelief, God gave him a sign. A young maiden would conceive and give birth, but before her child would grow old enough to know right and wrong, Judah would see defeat (Isa. 7:10-17). (The Hebrew word for "young maiden" can also mean "virgin," and as such became a prophecy for yet another birth, the virgin birth of the Messiah.)

In the next chapter of the narrative, Isaiah's wife, a prophetess, (8:3)conceived and gave birth to a child (Maher-Shalal-Hash-Baz) whose name means "quick to plunder, swift to the spoil." God told Isaiah that before this child could say, "My father," Judah would be conquered by Assyria (8:1-4). The couple's first child was named Shear-Jashub, which means "a remnant will return" (see 7:3; 10:21).

Instead of trusting God, Ahaz turned to Assyria for help. Israel in the north, with Syria, attacked Judah and, although they could not take Jerusalem, the damage they caused was great. Assyria eventually defeated the northern kingdom, placed a pro-Assyrian puppet on the northern throne, and when he rebelled the nation was finally destroyed.

In order to prevent further uprising, Assyria dispersed most of the Israelites all over the world. If a nation cannot stand united, it cannot rebel. Other peoples were brought into the land and they intermarried with the remaining Israelites (2

Kings 17:24-41). It was these mixed marriages that produced the Samaritans, Jewish "half-breeds" despised by the Jews of Jesus' day.

Ahaz continued his apostasy from the true God despite all of Isaiah's prophetic work. He built an altar in imitation of one he saw in Damascus and put it in the Temple. He removed many of the valuables there to pay the Assyrians tribute, and continually brought pagan practices into the nation.

When Ahaz died, his son Hezekiah took the throne (2 Kings 18–20; 2 Chron. 29–32; Isa. 36–39). Hezekiah had seen Israel destroyed by the Assyrians because of their sin, and his father had marched Judah full speed down the same path. Instead of following this poor example, Hezekiah brought about tremendous religious reform and revival. He destroyed the high places of idol worship and the images of false gods. He purified the Temple and offered worship to the true God. The nation held the Passover celebration for the first time in many years, and even invited many from northern Israel. Hezekiah reorganized the priests and Levites, and set about to regularly observe the Lord's feasts once again.

Hezekiah was more true to the Lord than any king had been since David and Solomon. Surprisingly, we read of little contact between Hezekiah and Isaiah, but Isaiah had opposed Ahaz and was active during Hezekiah's time. We can safely assume that the two did work together, probably quite closely. Surely the success of the revival must be credited partially to Isaiah's preaching.

After fourteen years of rule, Hezekiah became very ill. Isaiah told him he was to die, but when Hezekiah prayed, God promised that He would remove the Assyrian threat and give Hezekiah fifteen more years.

When the Assyrian king died in 705 B.C., the nations he had subjugated rebelled. Judah joined in the rebellion with some measure of success. But the Assyrian king, Sennacherib, soon subdued many of these nations, and brought a siege against Jerusalem. Hezekiah sought help from God, and Isaiah told him that the Lord would intervene. The following morning 185 thousand Assyrians were found dead. Either God's angel simply slew them, or perhaps He caused a disease to come from the swampy mouth of the Nile, often noted as a breeding ground of diseases. Speculation aside, the fact remains that because Hezekiah sought help from the Lord, God slew the enemy. Sennacherib returned home and was murdered by two of his sons.

The last time we read of Isaiah is when Hezekiah showed envoys from Babylon all of his riches. Isaiah told him that some day all of Hezekiah's wealth and family would be taken captive to Babylon. The rest of Hezekiah's reign was in peace and prosperity. But when he died and his son Manasseh ruled, the situation deteriorated. Manasseh reinstated all the pagan practices which his father had abolished. His sinning was so great that God promised to bring judgment against the nation, a judgment which paralleled Isaiah's prophecies to Hezekiah of coming punishment. There was no longer any hope for the immediate restoration of the kingdom. Destruction was coming (2 Kings 21:12-18). About a century later, Judah was taken captive by the Babylonians and Isaiah's prophecies were fulfilled.

Such were the times of Isaiah. It was to such extremes of religious instability that he addressed his message, prophesying more than sixty years until, according to tradition, he was martyred during the reign of Manasseh, one of the most wicked kings recorded in the Old Testament. Tradition says the prophet was fleeing from the soldiers of the king and hid in a hollow tree, hoping to escape. But the soldiers, knowing he was in the tree, sawed the tree down and the prophet was sawed in half.

The life and writings of Isaiah teach us that God is a holy God. The account in Isaiah 6 of his commission brings this point out clearly. In a vision, Isaiah saw God upon His throne. Above Him the seraphs flew, with wings covering their faces in humility, crying out, "Holy, holy, holy is the Lord Almighty; the whole earth is full of his glory." At their cry the Temple shook and was filled with smoke (6:3-4). The basic idea behind the word "holy" is "separation." God is holy in that He is separate from all else; He is infinitely higher than everything else. "To whom will you compare me? Or who is my equal?" God asked Isaiah (40:25). The answer of course is, "No one."

What a contrast this must have been to Isaiah's world. All around there was sin, or at best mere lip service. And when things did get better, sooner or later they would get worse. Being privy to the holiness of God must have strengthened Isaiah's faithfulness to his call.

Isaiah's response to seeing the holy God is instructive. "Woe to me!" he cried. "I am ruined! For I am a man of unclean lips, and I live among a people of unclean lips, and my eyes have seen the

King, the Lord Almighty" (6:5). When face to face with the Holy God, our only response is humility and realization of our sin.

Once, after Jesus performed a miracle, Peter realized his Master's power, and fell to his knees saying, "Go away from me, Lord; I am a sinful man!" (Luke 5:8). When Thomas was confronted with the risen Lord he could but cry out in all humility and reverence, "My Lord and my God!" (John 20:28).

The New Testament teaches that God is our Father; there is to be an intimacy in our relationship to Him. However, this familiarity can be taken too far. Although God is our Father, we must never forget that He is also the Holy Holy Holy Lord God Almighty, Master of all things. Our relationship is intimate but not irreverent, and certainly not flippant. We have all heard prayers that betray flippancy where there should have been godly fear. We would do well to fall at the feet of our loving heavenly Father in true fear; in fact, we dare do nothing else. He is our Father; He is also our God.

In addition to the holiness of God, the life of Isaiah demonstrates that God is a God of wrath. Because God is holy, He can have nothing to do with sin. In fact, God would compromise His holiness if He let sin go unpunished. This He will not and cannot do. Sin must be punished.

Some say that the God of the New Testament is a loving God, but the God of the Old Testament is mean and cruel. Those who say this have not fully grasped the full implication of God's holiness, and therefore they do not understand the wrathful consequences of sin. God's holiness demanded punishment for Judah's sins, but God also proved he is compassionate and forgiving (Isa. 1:18), able to put our sins behind His back (38:17), to remember them no more (43:25). When Judah had been punished, God promised to do a "new thing" (43:19): Judah would sing a new song (42:10), be called by a new name (62:2), and live on a new earth (65:17). God's forgiveness and restoration would be so complete that everything would be brand new. The God of the Old Testament is also a God of love and compassion.

We too should be as Isaiah was—long-term optimists. Especially in the first half of his book, Isaiah intermixes warnings of imminent destruction with promises of future salvation. Things may look bad to us now. The threat of global annihilation is always present. Millions of people are going hungry or dying every day. The church in many areas of the world is so dead that it seems to be of little worth. Christians in many areas of the world are being martyred because they worship the Lord. The list of the world's woes seems endless. Yet, somewhere down the road, stands God and His salvation. We who are children of God know for a fact that in the end our Lord will be victorious, and if we remain faithful, we will be victorious with Him.

This is the message of the book of Revelation. Its purpose is not to give us a road map into the future, despite what is often taught. Eschatology is ethical; knowledge of the future is to show us how to behave now. Things may look dark, but Christians know that they will win in the end. Be faithful to the calling; be a long-term optimist, for the Lord is coming again, and coming as the victor.

Isaiah's prophecy points out that no nation is above divine punishment. Judah was God's chosen people; they were His special project. Still God sent them into captivity and allowed them to be persecuted. No nation is above punishment for its sins, regardless of how much good they have done. God sent the wicked, sinful Assyrians against Israel, and the godless Babylonians against Judah. Will God hesitate to use another godless nation to punish modern nations whose sins are an abomination to Him?

Isaiah saw that formal religion with no real conviction is utterly worthless. The people of Judah paid lip service to God on the Sabbath but did what they pleased the rest of the week (1:15); they might have been better off if they had never observed the Sabbath (1:13-14). An empty following of religious ritual carries no favor with God. Rather, what God wishes is that once we have prayed, we live as if we have been speaking with the living God and indeed we have (Isa. 1:10-17; 29:13; 58:1-14; see also Hos. 6:6; Amos 5:21-24; Mic. 6:6-8). Merely going to church and leaving at the pew what we have learned will count for nothing when we stand before the throne of the Lord God Almighty.

One final point about Isaiah deserves attention. Isaiah's preaching was visual, emphasizing imminent destruction and eventual salvation. This is why he named his sons "quick to plunder, swift to the spoil," and "a remnant will return." Note also that Isaiah's own name means "the Lord saves." His sons were visual reminders to the people that the Babylonians were coming soon, but after a while the Jews would return from exile.

Another reminder was given when God told Isaiah to walk around "stripped and barefoot" for three years as a visual commentary to the nation that they would soon be marched off into captivity, stripped and barefoot (Isa. 20).

When we teach and preach, sometimes simple words are not enough. We need to keep in mind the force of the enacted parable. Unfortunately, many teachers and pastors are unused to theatrics, and this type of teaching often has a bad name. When done properly, however, acting out a message in an unusual manner can have tremendous impact, and be easily remembered.

Discussion Questions

1. The people of Judah were constantly fluctuating in their obedience to God. In the end, this type of instability resulted in their ruin. What types of fluctuation and instability mark a Christian's life? How can this be overcome?

2. When Hezekiah trusted in the Lord, he was rewarded. When Ahaz trusted in Assyria, he was punished. Give two examples of how, in your personal lives, you have trusted in your "Assyria" and been defeated, and in God and have been kept safe.

3. How can we impress upon those around us that God is a holy God? Be creative in your suggestions.

4. Have you ever been confronted with God's holiness? How did you respond?

5. Think of an example that would help others

understand the relationship between God's holiness and His wrath.

6. When was the last time things looked bleak, but down the way you could see God's light at the end of the tunnel? How did recognizing the promise of future hope help you cope with the present situation?

7. "God would never let godless Russia conquer a Christian nation like America." How would you respond to this statement?

8. How does Isaiah's warning against empty religious ritual relate to you and your church?

9. What are some creative ways in which you can "jazz up" your teaching so it has creative impact?

Note
1. Ronald Youngblood, *Themes from Isaiah* (Ventura, CA: Regal Books, 1984), p. 8.

Chapter 11

Jeremiah: The Prophet Who Would Not Compromise

Jeremiah prophesied during one of the most interesting periods of Old Testament history. He lived through the final destruction of Judah, ministering to its last five kings. He saw his country crushed between superpowers. He was part of its greatest revival, and witness to its final apostasy. Through it all, he proclaimed his message without compromising with the world.

Luckily, we know a great deal about the man Jeremiah. Through the heartfelt writings recorded in the book that bears his name, Jeremiah lets us see quite clearly into his heart and life.

As we saw in the previous chapter, King Manasseh undid all the good achieved by Hezekiah. He promoted pagan worship and killed Isaiah. Jeremiah was born during this time, probably in the 640s B.C. He was from a priestly family in Anathoth, a small village three miles northeast of Jerusalem.

Because of Manasseh's sin, God declared that judgment was coming (2 Kings 21:10-15; Jer. 15:4). Manasseh's son and successor was assassinated after a two-year rule, and his grandson Josiah became king at the age of eight. Contrary to his father and grandfather, Josiah did only what was good in the eyes of the Lord for his thirty-one-year rule (2 Kings 22:1–23:30). He instituted the most sweeping reform Judah had ever seen. Because of this, God promised to delay the coming punishment until after his death.

When Josiah was twenty he began destroying all the places of false worship and killing the pagan priests. When he was twenty-six he purified the Temple and held the greatest Passover the land had seen since the time of Samuel. The accounts of this time testify to the depths to which Judah had fallen. It is clear why God's punishment was inevitable. In the thirteenth year of Josiah's reign, Jeremiah began his prophetic ministry. (He was probably accompanied by the prophets Nahum, Habakkuk, and Zephaniah.)

Jeremiah was quite young, about twenty, when God called him. In fear, Jeremiah responded, "I do not know how to speak; I am only a child" (Jer. 1:6). But the Lord replied that He would give Jeremiah the words and protect him (1:7-19).

What words of encouragement are these to those who proclaim the Word of the Lord today. God Himself will be the speech writer and protector of those He calls.

Jesus promised that when we must testify to our faith, the Holy Spirit will give us the words (Mark 13:11) so that no one can resist or contradict us (Luke 21:15). Just a few months after

Jesus made this promise, Peter and John stood before the Sanhedrin and, filled with the Holy Spirit, gave their defense ending with the words, "Judge for yourselves whether it is right in God's sight to obey you rather than God. For we cannot help speaking about what we have seen and heard" (Acts 4:19-20).

When God calls us to a task He does not send us out empty-handed. We become instruments of His power, His words, His grace. When we go into spiritual battle without the full armor, it is only in an effort to fight by our own ability, our own words, our own strength. But God is a good General, supplying His troops with the necessary weaponry. So take heart and fight the battle joyously, for we know that through God's help we will win.

God's call to Jeremiah was really the second of two events. God said to Jeremiah, "Before I formed you in the womb I knew you, before you were born I set you apart; I appointed you as a prophet to the nations" (Jer. 1:5). A few others have had the privilege of a call from birth. Paul was "set . . . apart from birth" (Gal. 1:15). John the Baptist was filled with the Holy Spirit from birth (Luke 1:11-17). The psalmist's life was planned before he was born (Ps. 139:13-16). The servant of the Lord in Isaiah was "formed . . . in the womb to be [God's] servant" (Isa. 49:5).

Some people seem to have always known what the Lord desired for them. Ever since their youth they knew they were to be a pastor, teacher, missionary, dentist. But God does not call all His children in this way. In fact, sometimes God offers a variety of possible directions; any of them is within His will. No matter how God chooses to call us, the important thing is that we respond in obedience. Despite the method of his calling, each of us is in fact called. All we are required to do is to be obedient.

God told Jeremiah that Judah would be destroyed by Babylon as punishment for their sins, especially those of Manasseh. Even though the people rejected his message, Jeremiah still proclaimed God's word boldly and faithfully, without compromising his message to fit what the people wanted to hear. The church today has a message which the world does not particularly want to hear, and which many in the church do not want to proclaim. The question for today is, "Will the church follow the example of Jeremiah, preaching the uncompromising message of God, relying on divine strength and protection?"

Judah sat right in the middle of conflicts between three superpowers: Egypt to the south, Assyria and Babylonia to the north. With the Mediterranean Sea to the west, and desert to the east, the narrow land of Palestine was part of the buffer between the superpowers, and as such was often a mere pawn in their battle plans. During Josiah's reign, Babylon had gained some power over Assyria. Josiah tried to prevent the Egyptian and Assyrian armies from joining forces against Babylon and he was killed in battle.

In contrast to Josiah, who had done only good in the eyes of the Lord, his three sons and one grandson did nothing but evil, trying to secure Judah's freedom through human means. During this time Jeremiah proclaimed his message with great fervor. Jehoahaz, Josiah's middle son, was not righteous like his father and, therefore, Jeremiah prophesied that he would die in captivity (Jer. 22:11-17). After three months of rule, he was taken captive to Egypt.

Pharaoh then put Josiah's eldest son Eliakim on the throne and changed his name to Jehoiakim. Jehoiakim was pro-Egyptian, but Jeremiah knew that Babylon was God's chosen agent of punishment. Jehoiakim was relying on human might, whereas Jeremiah preached divine sovereignty. Thus the stage was set for fierce opposition between king and prophet.

And what was Jeremiah's message? That Judah had sinned against God (2:1–3:5; 5:1-13; 7:30–9:6,13-21; 16:19–17:4). That politically, morally, and spiritually the kings, officials, and common people were bankrupt. Judah had forsaken God's law (9:13-16), had turned to idols (chaps. 7,10), had broken the covenant (11:1-17), and did not keep the Sabbath holy (17:19-27). Times were so bad that they could not even trust a brother (9:4) because there was not one honest person left (5:1). Judah had so little shame they had forgotten how to blush (6:15). Most disheartening of all, they no longer were in awe of God (2:19). Their persecution of Jeremiah speaks to their sad state of spiritual depravity. Jeremiah proclaimed that as punishment, Babylon was coming to take the people into captivity (1:15-16; 4:5-31; 5:14-17; 6:22-30; 13:15-27).

Jeremiah zeroed in on several special topics. One was that Judah was only paying lip service to God not obeying His commands (7:1-29). They stole, murdered, committed adultery, and worshiped Baal. But on the Sabbath they sought protection in the Temple, believing that God would never let His Temple be destroyed. "We are God's nation," they might have argued. "Look, here is His house of worship. Surely He will not allow a pagan nation to trample us underfoot." If Jeremiah were living today, it is doubtful that his condemnation of empty, ritualistic worship would be any different.

Jeremiah wished destruction upon his enemies (11:18-23; 18:18-23). This was especially true of the false prophets who were teaching wickedness (23:9-40), saying that Judah would not be taken captive (14:13-22; 27:14; 28:2), and that the nation should fight Babylon (29:24-32). But as is the case in the Psalms, Jeremiah's anger was not selfish but a righteous condemnation of those who would oppose the word of God. Surely Jeremiah himself hurt from their rejection and persecution. But it takes a special person to be angered for God's sake rather than for his own.

Jeremiah placed the responsibility for the nation's apostasy on the officials and kings (chap. 23). Positions of influence and authority require additional responsibility, and therefore additional culpability when leaders encourage their people to sin (see Jas. 3:1). Pastors and politicians alike will answer to the Lord for the results of their labors, whether good or bad.

Jeremiah spoke words of both imminent doom and future hope to the nations around Judah as well. (Jer. 3:6–4:2; 12:14-17; 25:15-38; 27:1-11; chaps. 47–51). Although his ministry was primarily to the southern kingdom, it did at times branch out to her neighbors, including Israel.

In the previous chapter we saw how Isaiah acted out his prophecy of Israel's coming captivity by walking about naked for three years (Isa. 20). This type of theatrics was common among prophets. Hosea, for example, married a prostitute to show that Israel had committed harlotry with foreign gods (Hos. 1:2-8; see also 3:1-5 and Ezek. 16). God told Ezekiel to draw a picture of Jerusalem, build miniature siege works against it, and then lie on his side for 430 days, symbolizing 430 years of captivity for Israel and Judah (Ezek. 4:1-8).

Likewise, God told Jeremiah to act out certain prophecies. Once he bought a linen belt, wore it for a while, and after a time buried it. Many days later, when he dug it up, it was, of course, ruined and useless, but Jeremiah wore it anyway. The message was that although God had bound Israel and Judah to Himself, they had disobeyed and become ruined and useless (Jer. 13:1-11; see also 18:1-23; 19:1-13).

Jehoiakim's pro-Egyptian rule had only encouraged the nation's disobedience. When Jeremiah preached that the people would be punished if they did not turn from their sin, the priests and prophets brought him to trial, wanting to kill him. As it turns out, the nation's officials stopped them. In the process, however, we see a dynamic picture of Jeremiah's courage and faith. When facing the officials, he did not back down. He said, "The Lord sent me to prophesy against this house and this city all the things you have heard. Now reform your ways and your actions and obey the Lord your God. Then the Lord will relent and not bring the disaster he has pronounced against you. As for me, I am in your hands; do with me whatever you think is good and right. Be assured, however, that if you put me to death, you will bring the guilt of innocent blood on yourselves and on this city and on those who live in it, for in truth the Lord has sent me to you to speak all these words in your hearing" (Jer. 26:12-15).

At another time, Jeremiah was put in stocks by the priest Pashbur because he proclaimed that Babylon would destroy Jerusalem. Upon his release, Jeremiah did not change his message, but instead told Pashbur that Babylon would indeed come and Pashbur would be taken into exile (20:1-6). Even under extreme pressure, Jeremiah did not compromise the message of God.

In Jehoiakim's fourth year, Jeremiah dictated all of his prophecies to his scribe Baruch. Because Jeremiah had been excommunicated from the Temple (36:5), Baruch was sent there to read the scroll. When the king got wind of this, he had the scroll read to him, burning it section by section after each had been read. Jeremiah dictated another copy, and pronounced God's judgment upon the king (chap. 45): His dynasty would be abolished, Jehoiakim would die and not even be buried (22:18-23; 36:30-31).

In 605 B.C. at the Battle of Carchemish, Egypt was defeated by the Babylonian Nebuchadnezzar, and Judah became a Babylonian vassal. Some of the Jews were deported to Babylon, probably including Daniel and Mordecai, Esther's cousin. Three years later Jehoiakim revolted, was defeated (2 Chron. 36:6), and killed in accordance with Jeremiah's prophecies.

His son Jehoiachin lasted only three months. That was long enough to earn God's displeasure though (Jer. 22:24-30). Because of Jehoiakim's revolt, Nebuchadnezzar lay siege to Jerusalem in

597 B.C. and after three months the king, Jehoiachin, surrendered (2 Kings 24:12). Jehoiachin
was taken to Babylon with the prophet Ezekiel and
ten thousand others, the Temple was plundered,
and Zedekiah was placed on the throne.

Zedekiah was Josiah's youngest son and therefore Jehoiachin's uncle. During his eleven-year
reign, he proved himself just as wicked as his
nephew. Although Zedekiah was pro-Babylonian,
many of his court officials were pro-Egyptian and
therefore were in head-to-head conflict with Jeremiah.

Jeremiah had always said that Babylon was
God's chosen instrument of punishment, but it
was now that this aspect of his message rang the
loudest. Jeremiah made a wooden yoke and went
before Zedekiah and some foreign envoys who
were plotting rebellion against Babylon. His message was that Judah and the other countries
would come under the Babylonian yoke. If they
would submit, God would let them stay in their
home country. But if they fought, they would lose
everything. The false prophet Hananiah broke Jeremiah's yoke, saying God would also break the
Babylonian yoke. Jeremiah replied that although
his wooden yoke had been broken, God would put
an iron yoke on the nations so they would not be
able to defeat the Babylonians. Hananiah paid the
price for his false prophecy with his death two
months later (Jer. 27–28).

Jeremiah continued to proclaim the coming
captivity as he wrote to those already held captive
in Babylon. He warned them not to believe the
false prophets who encouraged a fight against
Babylon. Rather, the exiles should settle down and

go on living in Babylon, for it would be seventy years before God would bring them back to Judah (chap 29; see chap. 24 and 25:1-14).

In 588 B.C. Zedekiah rebelled, and Nebuchadnezzar put Jerusalem under siege. Jeremiah continued to urge surrender to the Babylonians (21:1-10; 34:1-7,17-22). At one time during the siege, Babylon withdrew to fight the approaching Egyptian force. This "retreat" once again fueled the fires against Jeremiah. He was imprisoned because a guard thought he was deserting, but Zedekiah rescued him (chap. 37). Later the prophet was thrown into an empty well by a court official and left to starve to death because he was telling everybody to leave the city. Again, he was rescued by another official (chap. 38).

During the siege, Jeremiah bought some land in the Judean city of Anathoth, to show there was future hope for Judah. Someday they would return (chaps. 32–33). Jeremiah had all along prophesied that God's chosen people would return from captivity (5:18-19; 16:14-15; 23:3-8; 29:10-14; chaps 30–31). It must have been a pretty dramatic message coming as it did when the Babylonians were attacking the city walls.

In 586 B.C. the city was taken, just as Jeremiah had prophesied. Zedekiah was blinded and deported to Babylon (see 38:17-23; 39:7). The city was burned, more of the people deported, Gedaliah was appointed governor, and Jeremiah was allowed to stay. Seven months later Gedaliah was assassinated, and the murderers fled to Egypt, forcing Jeremiah and Baruch to go with them (2 Kings 24:20–25:26; Jer. chaps. 39–43; 52). The last we know of Jeremiah he was living in Egypt, pronouncing God's wrath upon the Jews there because of their unrepentant idolatry (chap. 44). According to tradition, Jeremiah was stoned to death by his countrymen, and that not without a touch of irony, for he died in the country which he had opposed his entire life.

Such was the life of Jeremiah, often called "the weeping prophet." He apparently had only a few friends (Jer. 29:29; 36:32; 38:7-13). God did not allow him to marry or have children (16:1), nor was he allowed to join in with any festive gathering (15:17; 16:8). His prayer life reveals a very lonely man prone to depression and discouragement (15:16-18; see also Lamentations). His own family (12:6) and hometown had turned against him (11:18-23). Because of his preaching he was ridiculed and persecuted (15:15-18; 20:7-18). At times it was so bad that Jeremiah wished he had never been born (15:10; 20:14).

Why did Jeremiah continue? Although he felt free to struggle with God and work through his emotions, he knew all along that God had called him to this task. He had a burning desire to see the Lord's justice (10:23-25; 12:1-4). In fact, even if Jeremiah tried not to preach, as he said, the Lord's word was "in my heart like a burning fire, shut up in my bones. I am weary of holding it in; indeed, I cannot" (20:9). If he tried not to preach, he would burst.

Anyone truly called of the Lord feels the same way when unable to obey the call. Life becomes a defeating vacuum without meaning. Nothing works. Frustration reigns. Jeremiah had to preach; for God's word was consuming his being, demanding to be proclaimed.

Do you feel a call to full-time ministry? Check your body temperature. If you are not boiling, then your call may be elsewhere. For the servant of the Lord is consumed with a burning desire to proclaim His truth.

Jeremiah may have been frustrated and depressed at times (20:7), but he was always faithful to proclaim God's message, even when that message foretold the exile of his beloved nation. He proclaimed His message clearly and without fear, despite what everybody else said. He did not compromise!

Jeremiah's resolve stands out above all else. Christians today live in an age of compromise. Just as Zedekiah's officials pressured the king to ignore the prophet's teaching, so also the world pressures us to drop our standards, to give in to their philosophies. Thirty years ago, how did the church view social drinking, dancing, movies, divorce, and many other issues? What is the view today? While there isn't necessarily a "Christian" stance on any of these issues, they do clearly show a gradual shifting of the church's values. Do we change because we think the world's values are more correct than those of our religious forefathers's? Or have our own religious values been eroded little by little, by society's continual pressure to compromise our values and standards?

We live in an age when well over a million unborn babies are aborted each year, many by irresponsible parents who are too promiscuous or too lazy to care. In a local paper an ad recently appeared: "Abortions, $150." It was followed by: "Divorces, $25" as if the two went hand in hand.

This year two million cases of child abuse will

be reported; in fact, child abuse is the number one cause of death for children under fifteen. We live in an age where 20 to 25-five percent of young female adults have been sexually abused, usually in the home.[1] In the not too distant future, homosexuals will be allowed to adopt and raise children. We live in an age when a four-year-old can turn on his parents' cable TV and watch *R*-rated movies and degenerating pornography.

Not only are churches conforming to the world's standards, but the word is running headstrong down its wicked path, unchecked for the most part by Christians. We must ask ourselves when this will stop. When will the secular erosion be blocked? When will the church put its foot down? Somewhere, someday, the line must be drawn. Compromise with the world must stop. Our churches and Christian schools must stand in condemnation of this sinfulness. We must. We must be the salt of the earth; preserving what is good, eliminating what is bad. We must take a stand, for if we do not we will cease to exist, a mere page in society's scrapbook of victories.

May God give us the words and the protection to proclaim His message that He gave Jeremiah. May we stand firm, proclaiming His truth in condemnation of the world, without giving in to the pressures of society. With the Lord's truth we dare not compromise.

Discussion Questions

1. How has God given you protection and a message when you needed it the most?

2. Did God call you to ministry early in childhood? Have you enjoyed it? What have you missed?

3. When you are attacked because you are a Christian, do you respond out of personal or divine indignation? What are some positive steps we can take to insure we do the latter?

4. Jeremiah's life was anything but happy. What does that say about the possibility of troubles in your own Christian walk?

5. To what specific task has God called you? (Remember, everybody is called.) How were you sure that you understood God properly?

6. What examples have you seen of the church's compromise with the world? How is the church failing to stand in judgment of the world's sin like Jeremiah did? What can we do to stem the tide?

Note
1. R. Sutherland, "Our Abused Children," *Focus on the Family*, February, 1984.

Chapter 12

Esther:
Stewardship of Beauty

Our final character in this study of Old Testament personalities is Esther. Her story is full of political intrigue and suspense. What may appear to be a string of mere coincidences is in reality a demonstration of God's behind the scenes work, controlling the situation, being faithful to bless the world through Abraham's descendants. Through Esther's story we encounter a woman who did not use her beauty for selfish gain, but was a faithful steward of the divine gift of beauty, using that gift as she played her part in God's redemptive drama.

Judah was in Babylonian captivity for seventy years. Eventually, Babylon was destroyed by the growing Persian empire under Cyrus the Great. By his edict many Jews were allowed to return home under the leadership of Sheshbazzar (Ezra 1:1-4; 6:3-5; 2 Chron. 36:22-23). However, many second- and third-generation Babylonian Jews were settled and prosperous; they chose to stay. Cyrus was followed by Cambyses II, Darius, Xerxes I (485-465 B.C.), and Artaxerxes II (465-425 B.C.). Most authorities believe that Xerxes I was Esther's husband, but others think it was Artaxerxes. ("Ahasuerus" is another name for the king, and is translated as such in some Bibles.) If it were Xerxes, as we will assume, then the second and third returns to Judah under the leadership of Ezra and Nehemiah (Ezra 7–10; Neh. 1–13) occurred after the events described in Esther's story. But either way, the book of Esther is concerned with the queen's bravery in the Persian court, and the threat of genocide for Abraham's descendants.

The book of Esther contains ten easily read chapters. Well-written and fascinating, the story encourages the reader to enjoy its romance firsthand. In a nutshell, it is the story of a Jewess who became queen of the Persian empire, and through her bravery and God's providence protected the Jewish nation from an attempt to end their race.

In his third year of reign, Xerxes held a great banquet. After seven days, while he was quite drunk, the king called for his queen, Vashti, to parade before the gathering in all her royal splendor. But she refused—one can only imagine why. The king therefore deposed her as an example to all the women in his realm that they must be obedient to their husbands (Esther 1:11-12); not quite in keeping with modern trends, but typical of those days.

A king must have a queen, and therefore a "beauty contest" was held. The most beautiful women from throughout his kingdom (which was most of the world) were brought to the palace. For a full year, they were given beauty treatments in preparation for the king. Among those chosen was a beautiful Jewish orphan named Hadassah. "Hadassah" means "myrtle." Perhaps because her Jewish ancestry was a secret, she also had a Persian name, Esther, meaning "star." Because her parents had died, she was raised by a cousin named Mordecai. They had been taken into Babylonian captivity along with King Jehoiachin and ten thousand others (see 2 Kings 24:14).

Esther was more than just another pretty face. When she went to the harem, the Bible says she won the favor of the man in charge (Esther 2:9). In fact, "Esther won the favor of everyone who saw her" (2:15). Four years after Vashti had been disposed of, Esther was summoned and the king was "attracted to Esther more than to any of the other women, and she won his favor and approval more than any of the other virgins" (2:17).

Esther was crowned queen. Although her beauty was obviously essential, Esther's character and personality had the depth and quality to endear her to others. She was open to advice (2:10,15,20) and, as we will see, was brave enough to lay her life on the line three times for the sake of her country. She was much more than just a pretty face.

Esther's cousin, Mordecai, often sat outside the palace (2:19). One day he overheard a plot to assassinate the king and told Esther who in turn told the king, crediting Mordecai. The instigators were hung, and the event was recorded in the king's records (2:19-23). This apparently irrelevant story introduces us to a major theme of the book of Esther. It is often pointed out that the story of Esther is very secular; the name of God never appears once. But just as we saw in the case of Jacob, God is the main character of the story. Was it by chance Esther was taken to the harem? Was it by chance that Mordecai happened to overhear the plot? Of course not. God's hand is clearly visible, for in His plan nothing "just happens." Mordecai's report will play an integral part in future events.

The second-in-command to Xerxes was Haman, the villain of the story, and an archetype of one of the most ignoble forms of bigotry—anti-semitism. Hitler was not the first to exercise unbridled hatred toward the Jews, and unfortunately will not be the last. Contrary to the king's command (see 3:1-2), Mordecai would not bow to Haman. This triggered Haman's bigotry and he plotted to kill all the Jews in Xerxes' kingdom. (He did not know Esther was Jewish.) He cast lots (called "pur") and selected the twelfth month of the year, Adar, to carry out his genocide.

Haman told the king that the Jews had different customs and were disobedient to his laws. An edict was given that on the thirteenth of Adar every single Jew in the kingdom was to be killed (Esther 3).

When Mordecai heard the edict he sent a message to Esther that she plead with the king. As Esther pointed out to her cousin, if someone went to the king unsummoned, he or she would die unless the king granted mercy, which, as seen in his treatment of Vashti, was not very often. Mordecai responded with one of the most beautiful statements on God's sovereignty in all of Scripture. "If you remain silent at this time, relief and deliverance for the Jews will arise from another place, but you and your father's family will perish. And who knows but that you have come to royal position for such a time as this?" (4:14).

The first half of the verse declares that God would faithfully protect Israel even if Mordecai himself did not know from where that protection would come. It took a real heart of faith to make a statement like that in the face of a royal edict. The second half of the verse is reminiscent of Joseph's statement to his brothers: "Do not be angry with yourselves for selling me here, because it was to save lives that God sent me ahead of you . . . to preserve for you a remnant on earth and to save your lives by a great deliverance" (Gen. 45:5,7).

Mordecai's statement is the only time in the book of Esther that God's activity is indirectly mentioned, but it is sufficient to support our argument that the book of Esther is concerned with individuals participating in God's sovereign control over history. God had made Esther queen so that through her he could protect His chosen nation.

Esther ordered that all the Jews fast for three days, as would she and her maidens. "When this is done, I will go to the king, even though it is against the law. And if I perish, I perish" (Esther 4:16). Esther was much more than just a pretty face; she had the courage and inner strength to risk her life for what she believed to be right. How many of us will die for a cause God has sent our way? Have we become so desensitized by the world that the thought of a little persecution makes us run from spiritual conflict?

Esther had to take the initiative. Despite Mordecai's claim (4:13-14), if anyone had a chance of surviving the program it would be the queen. Yet Esther was willing to take the initiative, to step out, and possibly die for her people.

Notice that Esther had to take the initiative. Despite Mordecai's claim (4:13-14), if anyone had a chance of surviving the program it would be the queen. But she was willing to take the initiative, to step out, and possibly to die for what she believed to be correct. How about us? Do we stand up for our convictions? When there is foul talk in the office, do we put our fingers in our ears and pretend that it never happened? When we hear Christians being ridiculed, do we put our cross inside our shirt and bury ourselves in our work? Or do we take the initiative, stand up for Christ, and defend our faith (1 Peter 3:15)? Very few modern-day Christians will face death if they are true to their beliefs. But western Christianity has become so complacent that it has forgotten the beneficial healing and strengthening that comes from spiritual attack. Remember Mordecai's challenge: You may have received that secretarial or business position because God wanted you to be influential there. If you fail to take the initiative, what will become of you and your faith?

Esther and all the Jews fasted for three days in preparation for her appearance before the king. She did not run in, arms flailing, totally unprepared for the onslaught. Likewise, if you know that your unsaved neighbors have recently lost their infant child in an automobile accident, do you go to them quoting Romans 8:28? Let's hope not. Nobody who is in the emotional throes of a child's death wants to hear that. No, you prepare yourself. You ask God for wisdom to handle the situation. Then and only then do you go to them, cry with them, hurt with them. Only when the initial shock is over do you share with them how God's Son also died; that He hurt then just as they do now. Esther knew that preparation was necessary in doing the Lord's work.

But did she do it alone? Was she a "super Christian"? No. She asked for the help and support of the believing community. Too many times people view Christianity as a religion solely for the individual. That the Christian is punished for his own sins and is saved on basis of his own faith is true, but a Christian is also saved into a community of Christians, the family of God, the Body of Christ. In this Body each part functions for the good of the Body as a whole. Each supports the Body, and in turn each is supported by the Body (1 Cor. 12:24-25; Eph. 4:12-13; Rom. 12:3-8). We are not to isolate ourselves from the Body (Heb. 10:25); radical individualism may be good Stoicism but it is terrible Christianity. Esther knew the value of group support and took advantage of it.

Finally, Esther herself fasted. Modern opinions on fasting range from "a silly, Jewish ritual" to "a demand for every Christian." The former is wrong because Christ fasted. The latter is wrong because it has no biblical support. Christians differ in their worship of the Lord. People are different, and their needs are met in various ways. However, every Christian needs to spend concentrated times in isolation with the Lord, and fasting is a discipline which has deeply enriched many lives. Maybe it will do the same for you.

So after making preparation, Esther went to

the king. Fortunately the king granted her audience. Xerxes asked what she wished, and Esther
invited him and Haman to a banquet. During the
banquet the king again asked what Esther
desired, and begging his patience she invited both
of them to yet another banquet to be held the next
day.

Esther is an example of beauty used properly,
not selfishly. She was beautiful both inside and
outside. Most of this world's "beautiful people" use
their God-given beauty for selfish purposes: dat-
ing, influence, promotion. In one sense there is
nothing wrong in this; we need to use all our abilities in pursuing the tasks God has laid before us.
But do we view our appearance in terms of stewardship? Esther must have. God gives us our faces
and bodies; we are to be stewards of all the gifts He
has given us, and are therefore responsible for
how we use them. To be sure, when we go in for a
job interview we make ourselves as presentable as
possible. Why? Are we seeking selfish approval as
an extension of our own desires? Or are we making the best use of God's gifts as His responsible
stewards? Are we using our looks to advance God's
kingdom or ours? It all comes down to our attitude. What controls our attitudes and actions
when appearances are involved? Esther used her
beauty to save her nation. What has your face done
lately?

When Haman left the banquet he was very
happy—until he passed Mordecai who again
refused to bow. That night, in consultation with
friends, Haman decided to build a gallows, and in
the morning ask the king permission to hang Mordecai. But it just so happened, the king could not

sleep that particular night. Instead of counting sheep he had the history of his reign read. When he came to the account of the assassination attempt that Mordecai foiled, Xerxes realized that he had not been rewarded.

Now it just so happened that at that very moment Haman arrived to make his request about the gallows. Before he could ask, however, Xerxes asked Haman how he thought the king should honor someone with whom he was pleased. Thinking that the king was speaking of himself, Haman answered that the man in whom the king delights should be given a royal robe, set on a royal horse, and be led through the city proclaiming that this is how the king honors men with whom he is pleased. Poor Haman. Instead of taking the royal ride himself as he had imagined, Haman was forced to lead Mordecai in such fashion. Haman was beginning to see his downfall (Esther 5–6).

As soon as this task was done, Haman rushed to Esther's banquet, not in a very festive mood. This time when the king asked Esther what she wished, she begged him to save her people from "this vile Haman" (7:6). In his wrath the king left to think, and Haman fell upon the couch where Esther was lying, pleading for his life. When Xerxes returned it looked as if Haman was molesting Esther. Haman's doom was pronounced; he was hanged on the gallows he had built for Mordecai. What a poignant illustration of divine irony. Not only did Mordecai receive the blessing Haman had planned for himself, but Haman was hung upon the gallows he had built with his own hands. As the text says later, "The evil scheme Haman had devised against the Jews . . . [came] back onto his own head" (Esther 9:25).

But the Jews' problems were not over. Once again Esther took the risk of going to the king uninvited, and once again he granted her an audience. Haman's planned massacre remained on the books and, according to law, no royal command could be revoked. So Xerxes gave another command which allowed the Jews to assemble for defense and to kill anyone who might attack them on the thirteenth day of Adar. This was the same day Haman had planned to kill them.

The Jews, of course, were ecstatic. In fact, the Gentiles in the region had come into such fear of them that many became Jewish proselytes in order to escape the coming blood bath. When the thirteenth came, five hundred of the Jews' enemies were killed. Upon Esther's request to the king the edict was extended another day. Three hundred more were killed including Haman's ten sons who were hanged. And all this was just in the Persian capital. Elsewhere in the kingdom seventy-five thousand were killed. In his own way, God had secured safety for His chosen people.

In order to celebrate, the Jewish feast called "Purim" was established, drawing its name from the "pur" which Haman cast. Every year it is held as a reminder of how the nation had been saved through the courage of Mordecai and Esther. But behind these two characters, behind all the "mere coincidences," lay God's hand, protecting His people, being faithful to His promises to Abraham.

Discussion Questions

1. Like Esther, Peter saw the importance of inward beauty (1 Pet. 3:3-4). What are ways in which outward beauty gets in the way of inward beauty? What are some guidelines you can set to keep the pursuit of outward beauty in its proper perspective?

2. In what little ways has God made you "lucky" this past week?

3. Give an example of how you have taken the initiative to stand up for what you believe.

4. When was the last time you got into trouble because you did not spend time with the Lord preparing for a trying situation? What would you do differently now if you had the chance to do it over?

5. When have you drawn strength from the Body of Christ to do an impossible task?

6. What discipline do you use to spend time in concentrated isolation with the Lord?

7. How has your appearance helped the cause of God's kingdom?

Epilogue

As we have seen, the Bible is not only a record of God's commands and precepts; it is a chronicle of people in relationship to their Creator, a testimony to God's concern for the individual as well as the race.

We have examined ten men and two women, each of whom performed a specific task in God's redemptive plan. Each was raised by God to become an instrument through which He shaped world and spiritual history. They have made us laugh and cry. They have taught and challenged us.

But if their lives sit idle on these pages, this book has been in vain. At the end of the Sermon on the Mount, Jesus tells the story of the wise and foolish builders. If I could be permitted to adapt it to our situation—if you do not put into practice what these 12 examples teach, it is as if you built a house on the shifting beach. But if you put into practice what they teach, it is as if you built a house on secure rock cliffs.

When the storms of life come, who will stand firm?

Bibliography

Bright, John, *A History of Israel* (Philadelphia: The Westminster Press, 1974).

Brueggemann, Walter, *Genesis* (Atlanta, GA: John Knox Press, 1982).

Campbell, Edward F., Jr., *Ruth* (Garden City, NY: Doubleday & Co. Inc., 1975).

Childs, Brevard S., *The Book of Exodus* (Philadelphia: The Westminster Press, 1974).

Feinberg, Charles L., *Jeremiah. A Commentary* (Grand Rapids: Zondervan, 1982).

Kidner, Derek, *Genesis* (Downers Grove, IL: Inter-Varsity Press, 1977).

LaSor, William Sanford, *Great Personalites of the Old Testament. Their Lives and Times* (Old Tappan, NJ: Fleming H. Revell Co., 1959).

Lockyer, Herbert, *All the Men of the Bible* (Grand Rapids: Zondervan, 1959).

Schultz, Samuel J., *The Old Testament Speaks* (New York: Harper & Row, 1970)

Von Rad, Gerhard., *Genesis* (Philadelphia: The Westminster Press, 1972, the revised edition).

Wood, Leon, *A Survey of Israel's History* (Grand Rapids: Zondervan, 1970).

Youngblood, Ronald, *Themes from Isaiah* (Ventura, CA: Regal Books, 1984).